I0297070

C-957 CAREER EXAMINATION SERIES

This is your PASSBOOK for...

Correction Officer Trainee

Test Preparation Study Guide Questions & Answers

NATIONAL LEARNING CORPORATION ®

212 Michael Drive, Syosset, NY 11791
(516) 921-8888 • www.passbooks.com
E-mail: info@passbooks.com

PUBLISHED IN THE UNITED STATES OF AMERICA

PASSBOOK® SERIES

THE *PASSBOOK® SERIES* has been created to prepare applicants and candidates for the ultimate academic battlefield – the examination room.

At some time in our lives, each and every one of us may be required to take an examination – for validation, matriculation, admission, qualification, registration, certification, or licensure.

Based on the assumption that every applicant or candidate has met the basic formal educational standards, has taken the required number of courses, and read the necessary texts, the *PASSBOOK® SERIES* furnishes the one special preparation which may assure passing with confidence, instead of failing with insecurity. Examination questions – together with answers – are furnished as the basic vehicle for study so that the mysteries of the examination and its compounding difficulties may be eliminated or diminished by a sure method.

This book is meant to help you pass your examination provided that you qualify and are serious in your objective.

The entire field is reviewed through the huge store of content information which is succinctly presented through a provocative and challenging approach – the question-and-answer method.

A climate of success is established by furnishing the correct answers at the end of each test.

You soon learn to recognize types of questions, forms of questions, and patterns of questioning. You may even begin to anticipate expected outcomes.

You perceive that many questions are repeated or adapted so that you can gain acute insights, which may enable you to score many sure points.

You learn how to confront new questions, or types of questions, and to attack them confidently and work out the correct answers.

You note objectives and emphases, and recognize pitfalls and dangers, so that you may make positive educational adjustments.

Moreover, you are kept fully informed in relation to new concepts, methods, practices, and directions in the field.

You discover that you are actually taking the examination all the time: you are preparing for the examination by "taking" an examination, not by reading extraneous and/or supererogatory textbooks.

In short, this PASSBOOK®, used directedly, should be an important factor in helping you to pass your test.

CORRECTION OFFICER TRAINEE

DUTIES

As a Correction Officer, under the direct supervision of a higher-ranking officer, you would be responsible for the custody and security, as well as the safety and well-being, of criminal offenders in State correctional facilities and correctional camps. You would supervise the movement and activities of inmates, make periodic rounds of assigned areas, conduct searches for contraband, maintain order within the facility, and prepare reports as necessary. You would advise inmates of the rules and regulations governing the operation of the facility and assist them in resolving problems. You would have a high degree of responsibility for your actions and decisions. You will play a large role in the rehabilitative process related to the incarcerated population. You may also be required to carry firearms in the performance of certain duties and to perform other related work as required.

As a Correction Officer Trainee you will be required to participate in, and satisfactorily complete all requirements of a training program before advancing to Correction Officer.

SCOPE OF THE EXAMINATION

The multiple-choice written test will cover knowledge, skills, and/or abilities in such areas as:

1. Observing and recalling facts and information;
2. Applying written information in a correctional services setting;
3. Preparing written material; and
4. Understanding and interpreting written material.

HOW TO TAKE A TEST

I. YOU MUST PASS AN EXAMINATION

A. WHAT EVERY CANDIDATE SHOULD KNOW

Examination applicants often ask us for help in preparing for the written test. What can I study in advance? What kinds of questions will be asked? How will the test be given? How will the papers be graded?

As an applicant for a civil service examination, you may be wondering about some of these things. Our purpose here is to suggest effective methods of advance study and to describe civil service examinations.

Your chances for success on this examination can be increased if you know how to prepare. Those "pre-examination jitters" can be reduced if you know what to expect. You can even experience an adventure in good citizenship if you know why civil service exams are given.

B. WHY ARE CIVIL SERVICE EXAMINATIONS GIVEN?

Civil service examinations are important to you in two ways. As a citizen, you want public jobs filled by employees who know how to do their work. As a job seeker, you want a fair chance to compete for that job on an equal footing with other candidates. The best-known means of accomplishing this two-fold goal is the competitive examination.

Exams are widely publicized throughout the nation. They may be administered for jobs in federal, state, city, municipal, town or village governments or agencies.

Any citizen may apply, with some limitations, such as the age or residence of applicants. Your experience and education may be reviewed to see whether you meet the requirements for the particular examination. When these requirements exist, they are reasonable and applied consistently to all applicants. Thus, a competitive examination may cause you some uneasiness now, but it is your privilege and safeguard.

C. HOW ARE CIVIL SERVICE EXAMS DEVELOPED?

Examinations are carefully written by trained technicians who are specialists in the field known as "psychological measurement," in consultation with recognized authorities in the field of work that the test will cover. These experts recommend the subject matter areas or skills to be tested; only those knowledges or skills important to your success on the job are included. The most reliable books and source materials available are used as references. Together, the experts and technicians judge the difficulty level of the questions.

Test technicians know how to phrase questions so that the problem is clearly stated. Their ethics do not permit "trick" or "catch" questions. Questions may have been tried out on sample groups, or subjected to statistical analysis, to determine their usefulness.

Written tests are often used in combination with performance tests, ratings of training and experience, and oral interviews. All of these measures combine to form the best-known means of finding the right person for the right job.

II. HOW TO PASS THE WRITTEN TEST

A. NATURE OF THE EXAMINATION

To prepare intelligently for civil service examinations, you should know how they differ from school examinations you have taken. In school you were assigned certain definite pages to read or subjects to cover. The examination questions were quite detailed and usually emphasized memory. Civil service exams, on the other hand, try to discover your present ability to perform the duties of a position, plus your potentiality to learn these duties. In other words, a civil service exam attempts to predict how successful you will be. Questions cover such a broad area that they cannot be as minute and detailed as school exam questions.

In the public service similar kinds of work, or positions, are grouped together in one "class." This process is known as *position-classification.* All the positions in a class are paid according to the salary range for that class. One class title covers all of these positions, and they are all tested by the same examination.

B. FOUR BASIC STEPS

1) Study the announcement

How, then, can you know what subjects to study? Our best answer is: "Learn as much as possible about the class of positions for which you've applied." The exam will test the knowledge, skills and abilities needed to do the work.

Your most valuable source of information about the position you want is the official exam announcement. This announcement lists the training and experience qualifications. Check these standards and apply only if you come reasonably close to meeting them.

The brief description of the position in the examination announcement offers some clues to the subjects which will be tested. Think about the job itself. Review the duties in your mind. Can you perform them, or are there some in which you are rusty? Fill in the blank spots in your preparation.

Many jurisdictions preview the written test in the exam announcement by including a section called "Knowledge and Abilities Required," "Scope of the Examination," or some similar heading. Here you will find out specifically what fields will be tested.

2) Review your own background

Once you learn in general what the position is all about, and what you need to know to do the work, ask yourself which subjects you already know fairly well and which need improvement. You may wonder whether to concentrate on improving your strong areas or on building some background in your fields of weakness. When the announcement has specified "some knowledge" or "considerable knowledge," or has used adjectives like "beginning principles of..." or "advanced ... methods," you can get a clue as to the number and difficulty of questions to be asked in any given field. More questions, and hence broader coverage, would be included for those subjects which are more important in the work. Now weigh your strengths and weaknesses against the job requirements and prepare accordingly.

3) Determine the level of the position

Another way to tell how intensively you should prepare is to understand the level of the job for which you are applying. Is it the entering level? In other words, is this the position in which beginners in a field of work are hired? Or is it an intermediate or advanced level? Sometimes this is indicated by such words as "Junior" or "Senior" in the class title. Other jurisdictions use Roman numerals to designate the level – Clerk I, Clerk II, for example. The word "Supervisor" sometimes appears in the title. If the level is not indicated by the title, check the description of duties. Will you be working under very close supervision, or will you have responsibility for independent decisions in this work?

4) Choose appropriate study materials

Now that you know the subjects to be examined and the relative amount of each subject to be covered, you can choose suitable study materials. For beginning level jobs, or even advanced ones, if you have a pronounced weakness in some aspect of your training, read a modern, standard textbook in that field. Be sure it is up to date and has general coverage. Such books are normally available at your library, and the librarian will be glad to help you locate one. For entry-level positions, questions of appropriate difficulty are chosen – neither highly advanced questions, nor those too simple. Such questions require careful thought but not advanced training.

If the position for which you are applying is technical or advanced, you will read more advanced, specialized material. If you are already familiar with the basic principles of your field, elementary textbooks would waste your time. Concentrate on advanced textbooks and technical periodicals. Think through the concepts and review difficult problems in your field.

These are all general sources. You can get more ideas on your own initiative, following these leads. For example, training manuals and publications of the government agency which employs workers in your field can be useful, particularly for technical and professional positions. A letter or visit to the government department involved may result in more specific study suggestions, and certainly will provide you with a more definite idea of the exact nature of the position you are seeking.

III. KINDS OF TESTS

Tests are used for purposes other than measuring knowledge and ability to perform specified duties. For some positions, it is equally important to test ability to make adjustments to new situations or to profit from training. In others, basic mental abilities not dependent on information are essential. Questions which test these things may not appear as pertinent to the duties of the position as those which test for knowledge and information. Yet they are often highly important parts of a fair examination. For very general questions, it is almost impossible to help you direct your study efforts. What we can do is to point out some of the more common of these general abilities needed in public service positions and describe some typical questions.

1) General information

Broad, general information has been found useful for predicting job success in some kinds of work. This is tested in a variety of ways, from vocabulary lists to questions about current events. Basic background in some field of work, such as sociology or economics, may be sampled in a group of questions. Often these are principles which have become familiar to most persons through exposure rather than through formal training. It is difficult to advise you how to study for these questions; being alert to the world around you is our best suggestion.

2) Verbal ability

An example of an ability needed in many positions is verbal or language ability. Verbal ability is, in brief, the ability to use and understand words. Vocabulary and grammar tests are typical measures of this ability. Reading comprehension or paragraph interpretation questions are common in many kinds of civil service tests. You are given a paragraph of written material and asked to find its central meaning.

3) Numerical ability

Number skills can be tested by the familiar arithmetic problem, by checking paired lists of numbers to see which are alike and which are different, or by interpreting charts and graphs. In the latter test, a graph may be printed in the test booklet which you are asked to use as the basis for answering questions.

4) Observation

A popular test for law-enforcement positions is the observation test. A picture is shown to you for several minutes, then taken away. Questions about the picture test your ability to observe both details and larger elements.

5) Following directions

In many positions in the public service, the employee must be able to carry out written instructions dependably and accurately. You may be given a chart with several columns, each column listing a variety of information. The questions require you to carry out directions involving the information given in the chart.

6) Skills and aptitudes

Performance tests effectively measure some manual skills and aptitudes. When the skill is one in which you are trained, such as typing or shorthand, you can practice. These tests are often very much like those given in business school or high school courses. For many of the other skills and aptitudes, however, no short-time preparation can be made. Skills and abilities natural to you or that you have developed throughout your lifetime are being tested.

Many of the general questions just described provide all the data needed to answer the questions and ask you to use your reasoning ability to find the answers. Your best preparation for these tests, as well as for tests of facts and ideas, is to be at your physical and mental best. You, no doubt, have your own methods of getting into an exam-taking mood and keeping "in shape." The next section lists some ideas on this subject.

IV. KINDS OF QUESTIONS

Only rarely is the "essay" question, which you answer in narrative form, used in civil service tests. Civil service tests are usually of the short-answer type. Full instructions for answering these questions will be given to you at the examination. But in case this is your first experience with short-answer questions and separate answer sheets, here is what you need to know:

1) Multiple-choice Questions

Most popular of the short-answer questions is the "multiple choice" or "best answer" question. It can be used, for example, to test for factual knowledge, ability to solve problems or judgment in meeting situations found at work.

A multiple-choice question is normally one of three types—

- It can begin with an incomplete statement followed by several possible endings. You are to find the one ending which *best* completes the statement, although some of the others may not be entirely wrong.
- It can also be a complete statement in the form of a question which is answered by choosing one of the statements listed.

- It can be in the form of a problem – again you select the best answer.

Here is an example of a multiple-choice question with a discussion which should give you some clues as to the method for choosing the right answer:

When an employee has a complaint about his assignment, the action which will *best* help him overcome his difficulty is to
A. discuss his difficulty with his coworkers
B. take the problem to the head of the organization
C. take the problem to the person who gave him the assignment
D. say nothing to anyone about his complaint

In answering this question, you should study each of the choices to find which is best. Consider choice "A" – Certainly an employee may discuss his complaint with fellow employees, but no change or improvement can result, and the complaint remains unresolved. Choice "B" is a poor choice since the head of the organization probably does not know what assignment you have been given, and taking your problem to him is known as "going over the head" of the supervisor. The supervisor, or person who made the assignment, is the person who can clarify it or correct any injustice. Choice "C" is, therefore, correct. To say nothing, as in choice "D," is unwise. Supervisors have and interest in knowing the problems employees are facing, and the employee is seeking a solution to his problem.

2) True/False Questions

The "true/false" or "right/wrong" form of question is sometimes used. Here a complete statement is given. Your job is to decide whether the statement is right or wrong.

SAMPLE: A roaming cell-phone call to a nearby city costs less than a non-roaming call to a distant city.

This statement is wrong, or false, since roaming calls are more expensive.

This is not a complete list of all possible question forms, although most of the others are variations of these common types. You will always get complete directions for answering questions. Be sure you understand *how* to mark your answers – ask questions until you do.

V. RECORDING YOUR ANSWERS

Computer terminals are used more and more today for many different kinds of exams.

For an examination with very few applicants, you may be told to record your answers in the test booklet itself. Separate answer sheets are much more common. If this separate answer sheet is to be scored by machine – and this is often the case – it is highly important that you mark your answers correctly in order to get credit.

An electronic scoring machine is often used in civil service offices because of the speed with which papers can be scored. Machine-scored answer sheets must be marked with a pencil, which will be given to you. This pencil has a high graphite content which responds to the electronic scoring machine. As a matter of fact, stray dots may register as answers, so do not let your pencil rest on the answer sheet while you are pondering the correct answer. Also, if your pencil lead breaks or is otherwise defective, ask for another.

Since the answer sheet will be dropped in a slot in the scoring machine, be careful not to bend the corners or get the paper crumpled.

The answer sheet normally has five vertical columns of numbers, with 30 numbers to a column. These numbers correspond to the question numbers in your test booklet. After each number, going across the page are four or five pairs of dotted lines. These short dotted lines have small letters or numbers above them. The first two pairs may also have a "T" or "F" above the letters. This indicates that the first two pairs only are to be used if the questions are of the true-false type. If the questions are multiple choice, disregard the "T" and "F" and pay attention only to the small letters or numbers.

Answer your questions in the manner of the sample that follows:

32. The largest city in the United States is
    - A. Washington, D.C.
    - B. New York City
    - C. Chicago
    - D. Detroit
    - E. San Francisco

1) Choose the answer you think is best. (New York City is the largest, so "B" is correct.)
2) Find the row of dotted lines numbered the same as the question you are answering. (Find row number 32)
3) Find the pair of dotted lines corresponding to the answer. (Find the pair of lines under the mark "B.")
4) Make a solid black mark between the dotted lines.

VI. BEFORE THE TEST

Common sense will help you find procedures to follow to get ready for an examination. Too many of us, however, overlook these sensible measures. Indeed, nervousness and fatigue have been found to be the most serious reasons why applicants fail to do their best on civil service tests. Here is a list of reminders:

- Begin your preparation early – Don't wait until the last minute to go scurrying around for books and materials or to find out what the position is all about.
- Prepare continuously – An hour a night for a week is better than an all-night cram session. This has been definitely established. What is more, a night a week for a month will return better dividends than crowding your study into a shorter period of time.
- Locate the place of the exam – You have been sent a notice telling you when and where to report for the examination. If the location is in a different town or otherwise unfamiliar to you, it would be well to inquire the best route and learn something about the building.
- Relax the night before the test – Allow your mind to rest. Do not study at all that night. Plan some mild recreation or diversion; then go to bed early and get a good night's sleep.
- Get up early enough to make a leisurely trip to the place for the test – This way unforeseen events, traffic snarls, unfamiliar buildings, etc. will not upset you.
- Dress comfortably – A written test is not a fashion show. You will be known by number and not by name, so wear something comfortable.

- Leave excess paraphernalia at home – Shopping bags and odd bundles will get in your way. You need bring only the items mentioned in the official notice you received; usually everything you need is provided. Do not bring reference books to the exam. They will only confuse those last minutes and be taken away from you when in the test room.
- Arrive somewhat ahead of time – If because of transportation schedules you must get there very early, bring a newspaper or magazine to take your mind off yourself while waiting.
- Locate the examination room – When you have found the proper room, you will be directed to the seat or part of the room where you will sit. Sometimes you are given a sheet of instructions to read while you are waiting. Do not fill out any forms until you are told to do so; just read them and be prepared.
- Relax and prepare to listen to the instructions
- If you have any physical problem that may keep you from doing your best, be sure to tell the test administrator. If you are sick or in poor health, you really cannot do your best on the exam. You can come back and take the test some other time.

VII. AT THE TEST

The day of the test is here and you have the test booklet in your hand. The temptation to get going is very strong. Caution! There is more to success than knowing the right answers. You must know how to identify your papers and understand variations in the type of short-answer question used in this particular examination. Follow these suggestions for maximum results from your efforts:

1) Cooperate with the monitor

The test administrator has a duty to create a situation in which you can be as much at ease as possible. He will give instructions, tell you when to begin, check to see that you are marking your answer sheet correctly, and so on. He is not there to guard you, although he will see that your competitors do not take unfair advantage. He wants to help you do your best.

2) Listen to all instructions

Don't jump the gun! Wait until you understand all directions. In most civil service tests you get more time than you need to answer the questions. So don't be in a hurry. Read each word of instructions until you clearly understand the meaning. Study the examples, listen to all announcements and follow directions. Ask questions if you do not understand what to do.

3) Identify your papers

Civil service exams are usually identified by number only. You will be assigned a number; you must not put your name on your test papers. Be sure to copy your number correctly. Since more than one exam may be given, copy your exact examination title.

4) Plan your time

Unless you are told that a test is a "speed" or "rate of work" test, speed itself is usually not important. Time enough to answer all the questions will be provided, but this does not mean that you have all day. An overall time limit has been set. Divide the total time (in minutes) by the number of questions to determine the approximate time you have for each question.

5) Do not linger over difficult questions

If you come across a difficult question, mark it with a paper clip (useful to have along) and come back to it when you have been through the booklet. One caution if you do this – be sure to skip a number on your answer sheet as well. Check often to be sure that you have not lost your place and that you are marking in the row numbered the same as the question you are answering.

6) Read the questions

Be sure you know what the question asks! Many capable people are unsuccessful because they failed to *read* the questions correctly.

7) Answer all questions

Unless you have been instructed that a penalty will be deducted for incorrect answers, it is better to guess than to omit a question.

8) Speed tests

It is often better NOT to guess on speed tests. It has been found that on timed tests people are tempted to spend the last few seconds before time is called in marking answers at random – without even reading them – in the hope of picking up a few extra points. To discourage this practice, the instructions may warn you that your score will be "corrected" for guessing. That is, a penalty will be applied. The incorrect answers will be deducted from the correct ones, or some other penalty formula will be used.

9) Review your answers

If you finish before time is called, go back to the questions you guessed or omitted to give them further thought. Review other answers if you have time.

10) Return your test materials

If you are ready to leave before others have finished or time is called, take ALL your materials to the monitor and leave quietly. Never take any test material with you. The monitor can discover whose papers are not complete, and taking a test booklet may be grounds for disqualification.

VIII. EXAMINATION TECHNIQUES

1) Read the general instructions carefully. These are usually printed on the first page of the exam booklet. As a rule, these instructions refer to the timing of the examination; the fact that you should not start work until the signal and must stop work at a signal, etc. If there are any *special* instructions, such as a choice of questions to be answered, make sure that you note this instruction carefully.

2) When you are ready to start work on the examination, that is as soon as the signal has been given, read the instructions to each question booklet, underline any key words or phrases, such as *least, best, outline, describe* and the like. In this way you will tend to answer as requested rather than discover on reviewing your paper that you *listed without describing*, that you selected the *worst* choice rather than the *best* choice, etc.

3) If the examination is of the objective or multiple-choice type – that is, each question will also give a series of possible answers: A, B, C or D, and you are called upon to select the best answer and write the letter next to that answer on your answer paper – it is advisable to start answering each question in turn. There may be anywhere from 50 to 100 such questions in the three or four hours allotted and you can see how much time would be taken if you read through all the questions before beginning to answer any. Furthermore, if you come across a question or group of questions which you know would be difficult to answer, it would undoubtedly affect your handling of all the other questions.

4) If the examination is of the essay type and contains but a few questions, it is a moot point as to whether you should read all the questions before starting to answer any one. Of course, if you are given a choice – say five out of seven and the like – then it is essential to read all the questions so you can eliminate the two that are most difficult. If, however, you are asked to answer all the questions, there may be danger in trying to answer the easiest one first because you may find that you will spend too much time on it. The best technique is to answer the first question, then proceed to the second, etc.

5) Time your answers. Before the exam begins, write down the time it started, then add the time allowed for the examination and write down the time it must be completed, then divide the time available somewhat as follows:
   - If 3-1/2 hours are allowed, that would be 210 minutes. If you have 80 objective-type questions, that would be an average of 2-1/2 minutes per question. Allow yourself no more than 2 minutes per question, or a total of 160 minutes, which will permit about 50 minutes to review.
   - If for the time allotment of 210 minutes there are 7 essay questions to answer, that would average about 30 minutes a question. Give yourself only 25 minutes per question so that you have about 35 minutes to review.

6) The most important instruction is to *read each question* and make sure you know what is wanted. The second most important instruction is to *time yourself properly* so that you answer every question. The third most important instruction is to *answer every question.* Guess if you have to but include something for each question. Remember that you will receive no credit for a blank and will probably receive some credit if you write something in answer to an essay question. If you guess a letter – say "B" for a multiple-choice question – you may have guessed right. If you leave a blank as an answer to a multiple-choice question, the examiners may respect your feelings but it will not add a point to your score. Some exams may penalize you for wrong answers, so in such cases *only*, you may not want to guess unless you have some basis for your answer.

7) Suggestions
   a. Objective-type questions
      1. Examine the question booklet for proper sequence of pages and questions
      2. Read all instructions carefully
      3. Skip any question which seems too difficult; return to it after all other questions have been answered
      4. Apportion your time properly; do not spend too much time on any single question or group of questions

5. Note and underline key words – *all, most, fewest, least, best, worst, same, opposite,* etc.
6. Pay particular attention to negatives
7. Note unusual option, e.g., unduly long, short, complex, different or similar in content to the body of the question
8. Observe the use of "hedging" words – *probably, may, most likely,* etc.
9. Make sure that your answer is put next to the same number as the question
10. Do not second-guess unless you have good reason to believe the second answer is definitely more correct
11. Cross out original answer if you decide another answer is more accurate; do not erase until you are ready to hand your paper in
12. Answer all questions; guess unless instructed otherwise
13. Leave time for review

b. Essay questions
1. Read each question carefully
2. Determine exactly what is wanted. Underline key words or phrases.
3. Decide on outline or paragraph answer
4. Include many different points and elements unless asked to develop any one or two points or elements
5. Show impartiality by giving pros and cons unless directed to select one side only
6. Make and write down any assumptions you find necessary to answer the questions
7. Watch your English, grammar, punctuation and choice of words
8. Time your answers; don't crowd material

8) Answering the essay question

Most essay questions can be answered by framing the specific response around several key words or ideas. Here are a few such key words or ideas:

M's: manpower, materials, methods, money, management
P's: purpose, program, policy, plan, procedure, practice, problems, pitfalls, personnel, public relations

a. Six basic steps in handling problems:
1. Preliminary plan and background development
2. Collect information, data and facts
3. Analyze and interpret information, data and facts
4. Analyze and develop solutions as well as make recommendations
5. Prepare report and sell recommendations
6. Install recommendations and follow up effectiveness

b. Pitfalls to avoid
1. *Taking things for granted* – A statement of the situation does not necessarily imply that each of the elements is necessarily true; for example, a complaint may be invalid and biased so that all that can be taken for granted is that a complaint has been registered

2. *Considering only one side of a situation* – Wherever possible, indicate several alternatives and then point out the reasons you selected the best one
3. *Failing to indicate follow up* – Whenever your answer indicates action on your part, make certain that you will take proper follow-up action to see how successful your recommendations, procedures or actions turn out to be
4. *Taking too long in answering any single question* – Remember to time your answers properly

IX. AFTER THE TEST

Scoring procedures differ in detail among civil service jurisdictions although the general principles are the same. Whether the papers are hand-scored or graded by machine we have described, they are nearly always graded by number. That is, the person who marks the paper knows only the number – never the name – of the applicant. Not until all the papers have been graded will they be matched with names. If other tests, such as training and experience or oral interview ratings have been given, scores will be combined. Different parts of the examination usually have different weights. For example, the written test might count 60 percent of the final grade, and a rating of training and experience 40 percent. In many jurisdictions, veterans will have a certain number of points added to their grades.

After the final grade has been determined, the names are placed in grade order and an eligible list is established. There are various methods for resolving ties between those who get the same final grade – probably the most common is to place first the name of the person whose application was received first. Job offers are made from the eligible list in the order the names appear on it. You will be notified of your grade and your rank as soon as all these computations have been made. This will be done as rapidly as possible.

People who are found to meet the requirements in the announcement are called "eligibles." Their names are put on a list of eligible candidates. An eligible's chances of getting a job depend on how high he stands on this list and how fast agencies are filling jobs from the list.

When a job is to be filled from a list of eligibles, the agency asks for the names of people on the list of eligibles for that job. When the civil service commission receives this request, it sends to the agency the names of the three people highest on this list. Or, if the job to be filled has specialized requirements, the office sends the agency the names of the top three persons who meet these requirements from the general list.

The appointing officer makes a choice from among the three people whose names were sent to him. If the selected person accepts the appointment, the names of the others are put back on the list to be considered for future openings.

That is the rule in hiring from all kinds of eligible lists, whether they are for typist, carpenter, chemist, or something else. For every vacancy, the appointing officer has his choice of any one of the top three eligibles on the list. This explains why the person whose name is on top of the list sometimes does not get an appointment when some of the persons lower on the list do. If the appointing officer chooses the second or third eligible, the No. 1 eligible does not get a job at once, but stays on the list until he is appointed or the list is terminated.

X. HOW TO PASS THE INTERVIEW TEST

The examination for which you applied requires an oral interview test. You have already taken the written test and you are now being called for the interview test – the final part of the formal examination.

You may think that it is not possible to prepare for an interview test and that there are no procedures to follow during an interview. Our purpose is to point out some things you can do in advance that will help you and some good rules to follow and pitfalls to avoid while you are being interviewed.

What is an interview supposed to test?

The written examination is designed to test the technical knowledge and competence of the candidate; the oral is designed to evaluate intangible qualities, not readily measured otherwise, and to establish a list showing the relative fitness of each candidate – as measured against his competitors – for the position sought. Scoring is not on the basis of "right" and "wrong," but on a sliding scale of values ranging from "not passable" to "outstanding." As a matter of fact, it is possible to achieve a relatively low score without a single "incorrect" answer because of evident weakness in the qualities being measured.

Occasionally, an examination may consist entirely of an oral test – either an individual or a group oral. In such cases, information is sought concerning the technical knowledges and abilities of the candidate, since there has been no written examination for this purpose. More commonly, however, an oral test is used to supplement a written examination.

Who conducts interviews?

The composition of oral boards varies among different jurisdictions. In nearly all, a representative of the personnel department serves as chairman. One of the members of the board may be a representative of the department in which the candidate would work. In some cases, "outside experts" are used, and, frequently, a businessman or some other representative of the general public is asked to serve. Labor and management or other special groups may be represented. The aim is to secure the services of experts in the appropriate field.

However the board is composed, it is a good idea (and not at all improper or unethical) to ascertain in advance of the interview who the members are and what groups they represent. When you are introduced to them, you will have some idea of their backgrounds and interests, and at least you will not stutter and stammer over their names.

What should be done before the interview?

While knowledge about the board members is useful and takes some of the surprise element out of the interview, there is other preparation which is more substantive. It *is* possible to prepare for an oral interview – in several ways:

1) Keep a copy of your application and review it carefully before the interview

This may be the only document before the oral board, and the starting point of the interview. Know what education and experience you have listed there, and the sequence and dates of all of it. Sometimes the board will ask you to review the highlights of your experience for them; you should not have to hem and haw doing it.

2) Study the class specification and the examination announcement

Usually, the oral board has one or both of these to guide them. The qualities, characteristics or knowledges required by the position sought are stated in these documents. They offer valuable clues as to the nature of the oral interview. For example, if the job involves supervisory responsibilities, the announcement will usually indicate that knowledge of modern supervisory methods and the qualifications of the candidate as a supervisor will be tested. If so, you can expect such questions, frequently in the form of a hypothetical situation which you are expected to solve. NEVER go into an oral without knowledge of the duties and responsibilities of the job you seek.

3) Think through each qualification required

Try to visualize the kind of questions you would ask if you were a board member. How well could you answer them? Try especially to appraise your own knowledge and background in each area, *measured against the job sought*, and identify any areas in which you are weak. Be critical and realistic – do not flatter yourself.

4) Do some general reading in areas in which you feel you may be weak

For example, if the job involves supervision and your past experience has NOT, some general reading in supervisory methods and practices, particularly in the field of human relations, might be useful. Do NOT study agency procedures or detailed manuals. The oral board will be testing your understanding and capacity, not your memory.

5) Get a good night's sleep and watch your general health and mental attitude

You will want a clear head at the interview. Take care of a cold or any other minor ailment, and of course, no hangovers.

What should be done on the day of the interview?

Now comes the day of the interview itself. Give yourself plenty of time to get there. Plan to arrive somewhat ahead of the scheduled time, particularly if your appointment is in the fore part of the day. If a previous candidate fails to appear, the board might be ready for you a bit early. By early afternoon an oral board is almost invariably behind schedule if there are many candidates, and you may have to wait. Take along a book or magazine to read, or your application to review, but leave any extraneous material in the waiting room when you go in for your interview. In any event, relax and compose yourself.

The matter of dress is important. The board is forming impressions about you – from your experience, your manners, your attitude, and your appearance. Give your personal appearance careful attention. Dress your best, but not your flashiest. Choose conservative, appropriate clothing, and be sure it is immaculate. This is a business interview, and your appearance should indicate that you regard it as such. Besides, being well groomed and properly dressed will help boost your confidence.

Sooner or later, someone will call your name and escort you into the interview room. *This is it.* From here on you are on your own. It is too late for any more preparation. But remember, you asked for this opportunity to prove your fitness, and you are here because your request was granted.

What happens when you go in?

The usual sequence of events will be as follows: The clerk (who is often the board stenographer) will introduce you to the chairman of the oral board, who will introduce you to the other members of the board. Acknowledge the introductions before you sit down. Do not be surprised if you find a microphone facing you or a stenotypist sitting by. Oral interviews are usually recorded in the event of an appeal or other review.

Usually the chairman of the board will open the interview by reviewing the highlights of your education and work experience from your application – primarily for the benefit of the other members of the board, as well as to get the material into the record. Do not interrupt or comment unless there is an error or significant misinterpretation; if that is the case, do not hesitate. But do not quibble about insignificant matters. Also, he will usually ask you some question about your education, experience or your present job – partly to get you to start talking and to establish the interviewing "rapport." He may start the actual questioning, or turn it over to one of the other members. Frequently, each member undertakes the questioning on a particular area, one in which he is perhaps most competent, so you can expect each member to participate in the examination. Because time is limited, you may also expect some rather abrupt switches in the direction the questioning takes, so do not be upset by it. Normally, a board member will not pursue a single line of questioning unless he discovers a particular strength or weakness.

After each member has participated, the chairman will usually ask whether any member has any further questions, then will ask you if you have anything you wish to add. Unless you are expecting this question, it may floor you. Worse, it may start you off on an extended, extemporaneous speech. The board is not usually seeking more information. The question is principally to offer you a last opportunity to present further qualifications or to indicate that you have nothing to add. So, if you feel that a significant qualification or characteristic has been overlooked, it is proper to point it out in a sentence or so. Do not compliment the board on the thoroughness of their examination – they have been sketchy, and you know it. If you wish, merely say, "No thank you, I have nothing further to add." This is a point where you can "talk yourself out" of a good impression or fail to present an important bit of information. Remember, *you close the interview yourself.*

The chairman will then say, "That is all, Mr. ______, thank you." Do not be startled; the interview is over, and quicker than you think. Thank him, gather your belongings and take your leave. Save your sigh of relief for the other side of the door.

How to put your best foot forward

Throughout this entire process, you may feel that the board individually and collectively is trying to pierce your defenses, seek out your hidden weaknesses and embarrass and confuse you. Actually, this is not true. They are obliged to make an appraisal of your qualifications for the job you are seeking, and they want to see you in your best light. Remember, they must interview all candidates and a non-cooperative candidate may become a failure in spite of their best efforts to bring out his qualifications. Here are 15 suggestions that will help you:

1) Be natural – Keep your attitude confident, not cocky

If you are not confident that you can do the job, do not expect the board to be. Do not apologize for your weaknesses, try to bring out your strong points. The board is interested in a positive, not negative, presentation. Cockiness will antagonize any board member and make him wonder if you are covering up a weakness by a false show of strength.

2) Get comfortable, but don't lounge or sprawl

Sit erectly but not stiffly. A careless posture may lead the board to conclude that you are careless in other things, or at least that you are not impressed by the importance of the occasion. Either conclusion is natural, even if incorrect. Do not fuss with your clothing, a pencil or an ashtray. Your hands may occasionally be useful to emphasize a point; do not let them become a point of distraction.

3) Do not wisecrack or make small talk

This is a serious situation, and your attitude should show that you consider it as such. Further, the time of the board is limited – they do not want to waste it, and neither should you.

4) Do not exaggerate your experience or abilities

In the first place, from information in the application or other interviews and sources, the board may know more about you than you think. Secondly, you probably will not get away with it. An experienced board is rather adept at spotting such a situation, so do not take the chance.

5) If you know a board member, do not make a point of it, yet do not hide it

Certainly you are not fooling him, and probably not the other members of the board. Do not try to take advantage of your acquaintanceship – it will probably do you little good.

6) Do not dominate the interview

Let the board do that. They will give you the clues – do not assume that you have to do all the talking. Realize that the board has a number of questions to ask you, and do not try to take up all the interview time by showing off your extensive knowledge of the answer to the first one.

7) Be attentive

You only have 20 minutes or so, and you should keep your attention at its sharpest throughout. When a member is addressing a problem or question to you, give him your undivided attention. Address your reply principally to him, but do not exclude the other board members.

8) Do not interrupt

A board member may be stating a problem for you to analyze. He will ask you a question when the time comes. Let him state the problem, and wait for the question.

9) Make sure you understand the question

Do not try to answer until you are sure what the question is. If it is not clear, restate it in your own words or ask the board member to clarify it for you. However, do not haggle about minor elements.

10) Reply promptly but not hastily

A common entry on oral board rating sheets is "candidate responded readily," or "candidate hesitated in replies." Respond as promptly and quickly as you can, but do not jump to a hasty, ill-considered answer.

11) Do not be peremptory in your answers

A brief answer is proper – but do not fire your answer back. That is a losing game from your point of view. The board member can probably ask questions much faster than you can answer them.

12) Do not try to create the answer you think the board member wants

He is interested in what kind of mind you have and how it works – not in playing games. Furthermore, he can usually spot this practice and will actually grade you down on it.

13) Do not switch sides in your reply merely to agree with a board member

Frequently, a member will take a contrary position merely to draw you out and to see if you are willing and able to defend your point of view. Do not start a debate, yet do not surrender a good position. If a position is worth taking, it is worth defending.

14) Do not be afraid to admit an error in judgment if you are shown to be wrong

The board knows that you are forced to reply without any opportunity for careful consideration. Your answer may be demonstrably wrong. If so, admit it and get on with the interview.

15) Do not dwell at length on your present job

The opening question may relate to your present assignment. Answer the question but do not go into an extended discussion. You are being examined for a *new* job, not your present one. As a matter of fact, try to phrase ALL your answers in terms of the job for which you are being examined.

Basis of Rating

Probably you will forget most of these "do's" and "don'ts" when you walk into the oral interview room. Even remembering them all will not ensure you a passing grade. Perhaps you did not have the qualifications in the first place. But remembering them will help you to put your best foot forward, without treading on the toes of the board members.

Rumor and popular opinion to the contrary notwithstanding, an oral board wants you to make the best appearance possible. They know you are under pressure – but they also want to see how you respond to it as a guide to what your reaction would be under the pressures of the job you seek. They will be influenced by the degree of poise you display, the personal traits you show and the manner in which you respond.

ABOUT THIS BOOK

This book contains tests divided into Examination Sections. Go through each test, answering every question in the margin. We have also attached a sample answer sheet at the back of the book that can be removed and used. At the end of each test look at the answer key and check your answers. On the ones you got wrong, look at the right answer choice and learn. Do not fill in the answers first. Do not memorize the questions and answers, but understand the answer and principles involved. On your test, the questions will likely be different from the samples. Questions are changed and new ones added. If you understand these past questions you should have success with any changes that arise. Tests may consist of several types of questions. We have additional books on each subject should more study be advisable or necessary for you. Finally, the more you study, the better prepared you will be. This book is intended to be the last thing you study before you walk into the examination room. Prior study of relevant texts is also recommended. NLC publishes some of these in our Fundamental Series. Knowledge and good sense are important factors in passing your exam. Good luck also helps. So now study this Passbook, absorb the material contained within and take that knowledge into the examination. Then do your best to pass that exam.

EXAMINATION SECTION

EXAMINATION SECTION
TEST 1

DIRECTIONS: Each question or incomplete statement is followed by several suggested answers or completions. Select the one that BEST answers the question or completes the statement. *PRINT THE LETTER OF THE CORRECT ANSWER IN THE SPACE AT THE RIGHT.*

Questions 1-6.

DIRECTIONS: Questions 1 through 6 are to be answered on the basis of the following list of items permitted in cells.

ITEMS PERMITTED IN CELLS	
comb	mop
spoon	towel
cup	letters
envelopes	pen
broom	soap
washcloth	money
writing paper	chair
books	dustpan
toothpaste	brushes
toothbrush	pencil

The questions consist of sets of pictures of four objects labeled A, B, C, and D. Choose the one object that is NOT in the above list of items permitted and mark its letter in the space at the right. Disregard any information you may have about what is or is not permitted in any institution. Base your answers SOLELY on the above list. Mark only one answer for each question.

1. 1.____

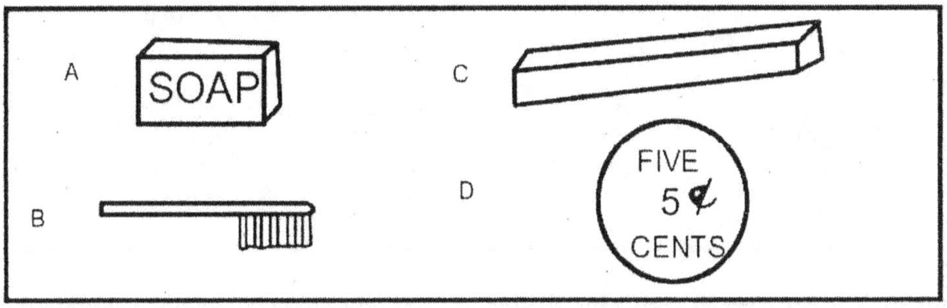

2. 2.____

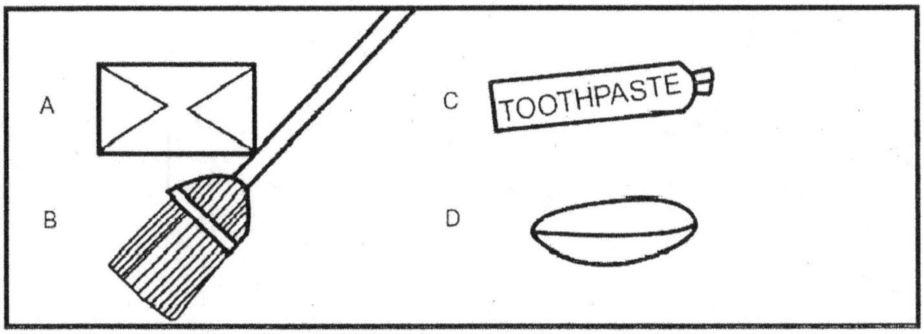

3. 3.____

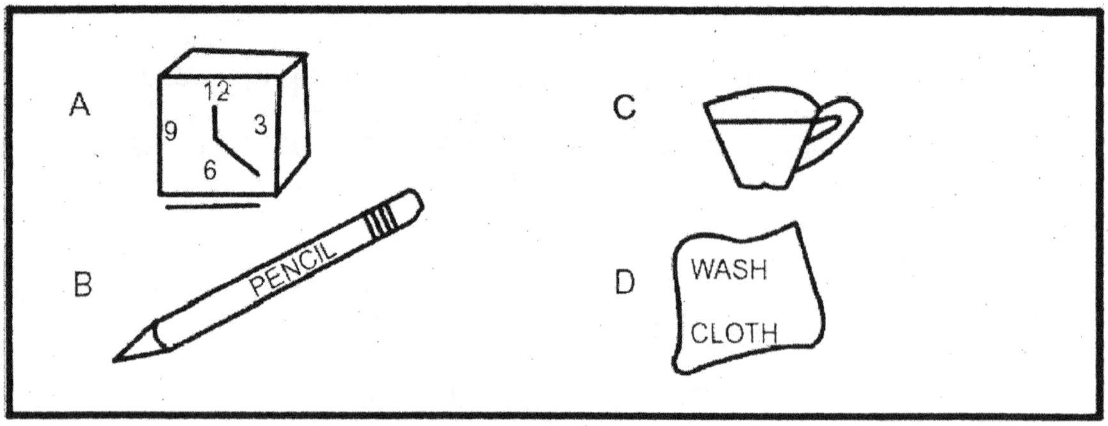

4. 4.____

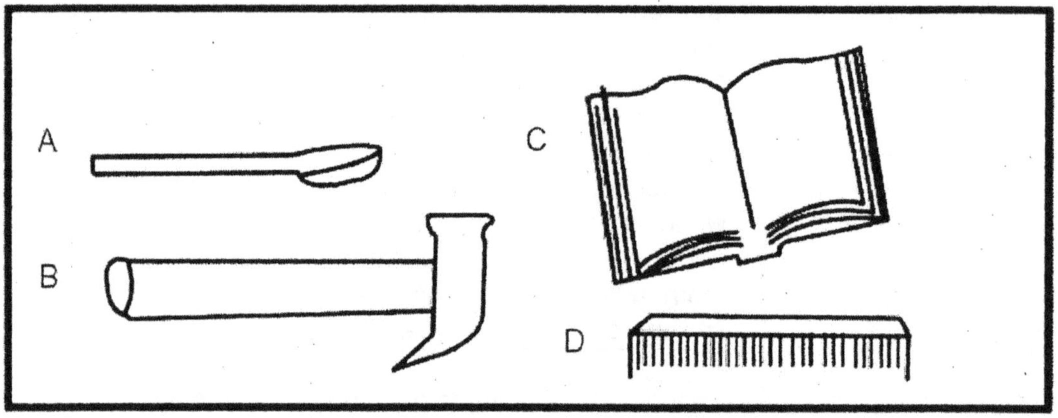

5. 5.____

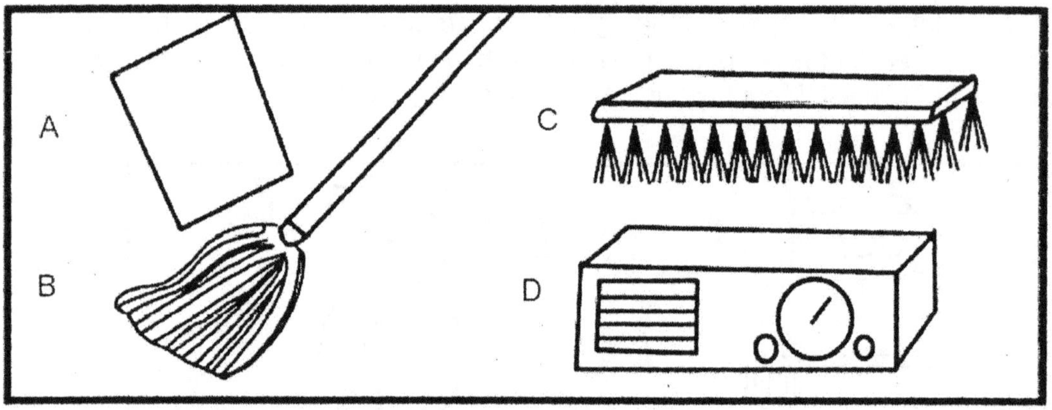

6. 6.____

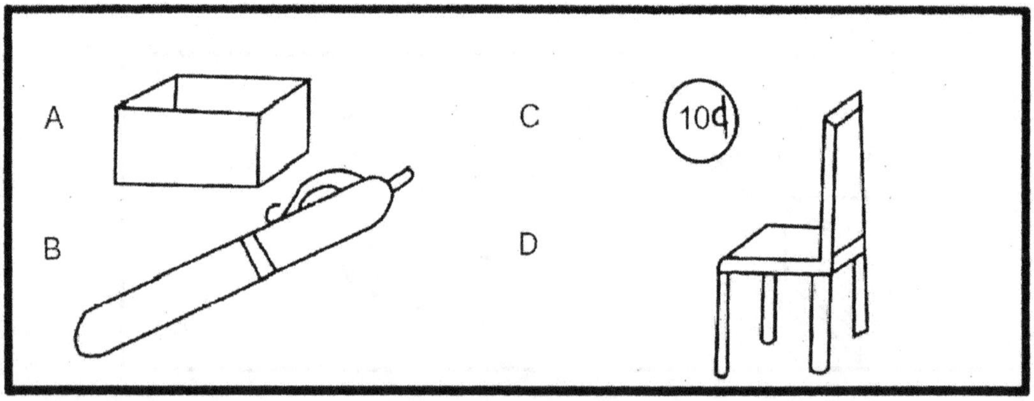

Questions 7-11.

DIRECTIONS: Questions 7 through 11 are to be answered on the basis of the following list showing the name and number of each of nine inmates.

1 - Johnson	4 - Thompson	7 - Gordon
2 - Smith	5 - Frank	8 - Porter
3 - Edwards	6 - Murray	9 - Lopez

Each question consists of 3 sets of numbers and letters.
Each set should consist of the numbers of three inmates and the first letter of each of their names. The letters should be in the same order as the numbers. In at least two of the three choices, there will be an error.

In the space at the right, mark only that choice in which the letters correspond with the numbers and are in the same order. If all three sets are wrong, mark Choice D in the space at the right.

SAMPLE QUESTION: A. 386 EPM
B. 542 FST
C. 474 LGT

Since 3 corresponds to E for Edwards, 8 corresponds to P for Porter, and 6 corresponds to M for Murray, Choice A is correct and should be entered in the answer space. Choice B is wrong because letters T and S have been reversed. Choice C is wrong because the first number, which is 4, does NOT correspond with the first letter of Choice C, which is L. It should have been T. If Choice A were also wrong, then D would have been the correct answer.

7. A. 382 EGS B. 461 TMJ C. 875 PLF 7.____

8. A. 549 FLT B. 692 MJS C. 758 GSP 8.____

9. A. 936 LEM B. 253 FSE C. 147 JTL 9.____

10. A. 569 PML B. 716 GJP C. 842 PTS 10.____

11. A. 356 FEM B. 198 JPL C. 637 MEG 11.____

Questions 12-16.

DIRECTIONS: Questions 12 through 16 are to be answered on the basis of the following passage.

Mental disorders are found in a fairly large number of the inmates in correctional institutions. There are no exact figures as to the number of inmates who are mentally disturbed—partly because it is hard to draw a precise line between "mental disturbance" and "normality"—but experts find that somewhere between 15% and 25% of inmates are suffering from disorders that are obvious enough to show up in routine psychiatric examinations. Society has not yet really come to grips with the problem of what to do with mentally disturbed offenders. There is not enough money available to set up treatment programs for all the people identified as mentally disturbed; and there would probably not be enough qualified psychiatric personnel available to run such programs even if they could be set up. Most mentally disturbed offenders are therefore left to serve out their time in correctional institutions, and the burden of dealing with them falls on correction officers. This means that a correction officer must be sensitive enough to human behavior to know when he is dealing with a person who is not mentally normal, and that the officer must be imaginative enough to be able to sense how an abnormal individual might react under certain circumstances.

12. According to the above passage, mentally disturbed inmates in correctional institutions 12.____

    A. are usually transferred to mental hospitals when their condition is noticed
    B. cannot be told from other inmates because tests cannot distinguish between insane people and normal people
    C. may constitute as much as 25% of the total inmate population
    D. should be regarded as no different from all the other inmates

13. The above passage says that today the job of handling mentally disturbed inmates is MAINLY up to 13.____

    A. psychiatric personnel
    B. other inmates
    C. correction officers
    D. administrative officials

14. Of the following, which is a reason given in the above passage for society's failure to provide adequate treatment programs for mentally disturbed inmates? 14.____

    A. Law-abiding citizens should not have to pay for fancy treatment programs for citizens.
    B. A person who breaks the law should not expect society to give him special help.
    C. It is impossible to tell whether an inmate is mentally disturbed.
    D. There are not enough trained people to provide the kind of treatment needed.

15. The expression *abnormal individual,* as used in the last sentence of the above passage, refers to an individual who is 15.____

    A. of average intelligence
    B. of superior intelligence
    C. completely normal
    D. mentally disturbed

16. The reader of the above passage would MOST likely agree that 16.____

    A. correction officers should not expect mentally disturbed persons to behave the same way a normal person would behave
    B. correction officers should not report infractions
    C. of the rules committed by mentally disturbed persons
    D. mentally disturbed persons who break the law should be treated exactly the same way as anyone else
    E. mentally disturbed persons who have broken the law should not be imprisoned

Questions 17-23.

DIRECTIONS: Questions 17 through 23 are to be answered on the basis of the roster of inmates, the instructions, the table, and the sample question given below.

Twelve inmates of a correctional institution are divided into three permanent groups in their workshop. They must be present and accounted for in these groups at the beginning of each workday. During the day, the inmates check out of their groups for various activities.

They check back in again when those activities have been completed. Assume that the day is divided into three activity periods.

ROSTER OF INMATES

GROUP X	Ted	Frank	George	Harry
GROUP Y	Jack	Ken	Larry	Mel
GROUP Z	Phil	Bob	Sam	Vic

The following table shows the movements of these inmates from their groups during the day. Assume that all were present and accounted for at the beginning of Period I.

		GROUP X	GROUP Y	GROUP Z
Period I	Check-outs	Ted, Frank	Ken, Larry	Phil
Period II	Check- ins	Frank	Ken, Larry	Phil
	Check-outs	George	Jack, Mel	Bob, Sam, Vic
Period III	Check-ins	George	Mel, Jack	Sam, Bob, Vic
	Check-outs	Frank, Harry	Ken	Vic

SAMPLE QUESTION: At the end of Period II, the inmates remaining in Group X were

A. Ted, Frank, Harry
B. Frank, Harry
C. Ted, George
D. Frank, Harry, George

During Period I, Ted and Frank were checked out from Group X. During Period II, Frank was checked back in, and George was checked out. Therefore, the members of the group remaining out are Ted and George. The two other members of the group, Frank and Harry, should be present. The correct answer is B.

17. At the end of Period I, the TOTAL number of inmates remaining in their own permanent groups was 17.____

A. 8 B. 7 C. 6 D. 5

18. At the end of Period I, the inmates remaining in Group Z were 18.____

A. George and Harry
B. Jack and Mel
C. Bob, Sam, and Vic
D. Phil

19. At the end of Period II, the inmates remaining in Group Y were 19.____

A. Ken and Larry
B. Jack, Ken, and Mel
C. Jack and Ken
D. Ken, Mel, and Larry

20. At the end of Period II, the TOTAL number of inmates remaining in their own permanent groups was 20.____

A. 8 B. 7 C. 6 D. 5

21. At the end of Period II, the inmates who were NOT present in Group Z were 21.____

A. Phil, Bob, and Sam
B. Sam, Bob, and Vic
C. Sam, Vic, and Phil
D. Vic, Phil, and Bob

22. At the end of Period III, the inmates remaining in Group Y were 22.___

A. Ted, Frank, and George
B. Jack, Mel, and Ken
C. Jack, Larry, and Mel
D. Frank and Harry

23. At the end of Period III, the TOTAL number of inmates NOT present in their own permanent groups was 23.___

A. 4 B. 5 C. 6 D. 7

24. Of the 100 inmates in a certain cellblock, one-half were assigned to clean-up work, and one-fifth were assigned to work in the laundry. 24.___
How many inmates were NOT assigned for clean-up work or laundry work?

A. 30 B. 40 C. 50 D. 60

25. A certain cellblock has a maximum capacity of 250 inmates. On March 26, there were 200 inmates housed in the cellblock. 12 inmates were added on that day, and 17 inmates were added on the following day. No inmates left on either day. 25.___
How many more inmates could this cellblock have accommodated on the second day?

A. 11 B. 16 C. 21 D. 28

KEY (CORRECT ANSWERS)

1. C
2. D
3. A
4. B
5. D

6. A
7. B
8. D
9. A
10. C

11. C
12. C
13. C
14. D
15. D

16. A
17. B
18. C
19. A
20. D

21. B
22. C
23. B
24. A
25. C

TEST 2

DIRECTIONS: Each question or incomplete statement is followed by several suggested answers or completions. Select the one that BEST answers the question or completes the statement. *PRINT THE LETTER OF THE CORRECT ANSWER IN THE SPACE AT THE RIGHT.*

Questions 1-5.

DIRECTIONS: Questions 1 through 5 are to be answered SOLELY on the basis of the Report of Offense that appears below.

REPORT OF OFFENSE		Report No.	*26743*
		Date of Report	*10-12*
Inmate	*Joseph Brown*		
Age	*27*	Number	*61274*
Sentence	*90 days*	Assignment	*KU-187*
Place of Offense	*R.P.W. 4-1*	Date of Offense	*10/11*
Offense	*Assaulting inmate*		
Details	*During 9:00 p.m. cellblock clean-up, inmate John Jones asked for pail being used by Brown. Brown refused. Correction officer requested that Brown comply. Brown then threw pail at Jones with intent to injure him and said he would "get" Jones. Jones not hurt.*		
Force Used by Officer	*None*		
Name of Reporting Officer	*R. Rodriguez*	No.	*C-2056*
Name of Superior Officer	*P. Ferguson*		

1. The person who made out this report is 1.____

   A. Joseph Brown
   B. John Jones
   C. R. Rodriguez
   D. P. Ferguson

2. Disregarding the details, the specific offense reported was 2.____

   A. insulting a fellow inmate
   B. assaulting a fellow inmate
   C. injuring a fellow inmate
   D. disobeying a correction officer

3. The number of the inmate who committed the offense is 3.____

   A. 26743
   B. 61274
   C. KU-187
   D. C-2056

4. The offense took place on 4.____

   A. October 11
   B. June 12
   C. December
   D. November 13

5. The place where the offense occurred is identified in the report as 5.____

   A. Brown's cell
   B. Jones' cell
   C. KU-187
   D. R.P.W., 4-1

6. Add $51.79, $29.39, and $8.98. 6.____
The CORRECT answer is

A. $78.97 B. $88.96 C. $89.06 D. $90.16

7. Add $72.07 and $31.54, then subtract $25.75. 7.____
The CORRECT answer is

A. $77.86 B. $82.14 C. $88.96 D. $129.36

8. Start with $82.47, then subtract $25.50, $4.75, and 35¢. 8.____
The CORRECT answer is

A. $30.60 B. $51.87 C. $52.22 D. $65.25

9. Add $19.35 and $37.75, then subtract $9.90 and $19.80. 9.____
The CORRECT answer is

A. $27.40 B. $37.00 C. $37.30 D. $47.20

10. Multiply $38.85 by 2; then subtract $27.90. 10.____
The CORRECT answer is

A. $21.90 B. $48.70 C. $49.80 D. $50.70

11. Add $53.66, $9.27, and $18.75, then divide by 2. 11.____
The CORRECT answer is

A. $35.84 B. $40.34 C. $40.84 D. $41.34

12. Out of 192 inmates in a certain cellblock, 96 are to go on a work detail and another 32 are to report to a vocational class. All the rest are to remain in the cellblock. 12.____
How many inmates should be left on the cellblock?

A. 48 B. 64 C. 86 D. 128

13. Assume that you, as a correction officer, are responsible for seeing that the right number of utensils are counted out for a meal. You need enough utensils for 620 men. One fork and one spoon are needed for each man. In addition, one ladle is needed for each group of 20 men. 13.____
How many utensils will be needed altogether?

A. 1240 B. 1271 C. 1550 D. 1860

14. Assume that you, as a correction officer, are supervising the inmates who are assigned to a dishwashing detail. There is a direct relationship between the amount of time it takes to do all the dishwashing and the number of inmates who are washing dishes. When two inmates are washing dishes, the job takes six hours. 14.____
If there are four inmates washing dishes, how long should the job take?
_______ hour(s).

A. 1 B. 2 C. 3 D. 4

15. Assume that you, as a correction officer, are in charge of supervising the laundry sorting and counting. You expect that on a certain day there will be nearly 7,000 items to be sorted and counted. 15.____
If one inmate can sort and count 500 items in an hour, how many inmates are needed to sort all 7,000 items in one hour?

A. 2 B. 5 C. 7 D. 14

16. A carpentry course is being given for inmates who want to learn a skill. The course will be taught in several different groups. Each group should contain at least 12 but not more than 16 men. The smaller the group, the better, as long as there are at least 12 men per group. If 66 inmates are going to take the course, they should be divided into 16.____

A. 4 groups of 16 men
B. 4 groups of 13 men and 1 group of 14 men
C. 3 groups of 13 men and 2 groups of 14 men
D. 6 groups of 11 men

Questions 17-21.

DIRECTIONS: Questions 17 through 21 are to be answered on the basis of the Fact Situation and the Report of Inmate Injury form below. The questions ask how the report form should be filled in, based on the information given in the Fact Situation.

FACT SITUATION

Peter Miller is a correction officer assigned to duty in Cellblock A. His superior officer is John Doakes. Miller was on duty at 1:30 P.M. on March 21, 2004, when he heard a scream for help from Cell 12. He hurried to Cell 12 and found inmate Richard Rogers stamping out a flaming book of matches. Inmate John Jones was screaming. It seems that Jones had accidentally set fire to the entire book of matches while lighting a cigarette, and he had burned his left hand. Smoking was permitted at this hour. Miller reported the incident by phone, and Jones was escorted to the dispensary where his hand was treated at 2:00 P.M. by Dr. Albert Lorillo. Dr. Lorillo determined that Jones could return to his cellblock, but that he should be released from work for four days. The doctor scheduled a re-examination for March 22. A routine investigation of the incident was made by James Lopez. Jones confirmed to this officer that the above statement of the situation was correct.

REPORT OF INMATE INJURY

(1) Name of Inmate ______ (2) Assignment ______
(3) Number ______ (4) Location ______
(5) Nature of Injury ______ (6) Date ______
(7) Details (how, when, where injury was incurred) ______

(8) Received medical attention: Date ______ Time ______
(9) Treatment ______
(10) Disposition (check one or more):
___ (10-1) Return to housing area ___ (10-2) Return to duty
___ (10-3) Work release ___ ___ days ___ (10-4) Re-examine in ___ days

(11) Employing reporting injury ______
(12) Employee's supervisor or superior officer ______
(13) Medical officer treating injury ______
(14) Investigating officer ______
(15) Head of institution ______

17. Which of the following should be entered in Item 1? 17.___

A. Peter Miller
B. John Doakes
C. Richard Rogers
D. John Jones

18. Which of the following should be entered in Item 11? 18.___

A. Peter Miller
B. James Lopez
C. Richard Rogers
D. John Jones

19. Which of the following should be entered in Item 8? 19.___

A. 2/21/04, 1:30 P.M.
B. 2/21/04, 2:00 P.M.
C. 3/21/04, 1:30 P.M.
D. 3/21/04, 2:00 P.M.

20. For Item 10, which of the following should be checked? 20.___

A. Only 10-4
B. 10-1 and 10-4
C. 10-1, 10-3, and 10-4
D. 10-2, 10-3, and 10-4

21. Of the following items, which one CANNOT be filled in on the basis of the information given in the Fact Situation? 21.___
Item _______.

A. 12 B. 13 C. 14 D. 15

Questions 22-25.

DIRECTIONS: Questions 22 through 25 are to be answered on the basis of the chart which appears on the following page. The chart shows an 8-hour schedule for 4 groups of inmates. The numbers across the top of the chart stand for hours of the day: the hour beginning at 8:00, the hour beginning at 9:00, and so forth. The exact number of men in each group is given at the lefthand side of the chart. An hour when the men in a particular group are scheduled to be OUT of their cellblock is marked with an X.

	8	9	10	11	12	1	2	3
GROUP Q 44 men	X		X			X		
GROUP R 60 men	X		X	X		X	X	
GROUP S 24 men	X				X			
GROUP T 28 men	X		X		X			

22. How many of the men were in their cellblock from 11:00 to 12:00? 22.____

    A. 60 B. 96 C. 104 D. 156

23. At 10:45, how many of the men were NOT in their cellblock? 23.____

    A. 24 B. 60 C. 96 D. 132

24. At 12:30, what proportion of the men were NOT in their cellblock? 24.____

    A. 1/4 B. 1/3 C. 1/2 D. 2/3

25. During the period covered in the chart, what percentage of the time did the men in Group S spend in their cellblock? 25.____

    A. 60% B. 65% C. 70% D. 75%

KEY (CORRECT ANSWERS)

1. C
2. B
3. B
4. A
5. D
6. D
7. A
8. B
9. A
10. C
11. C
12. B
13. B
14. C
15. D
16. B
17. D
18. A
19. D
20. C
21. D
22. B
23. D
24. B
25. D

EXAMINATION SECTION
TEST 1

DIRECTIONS: Each question or incomplete statement is followed by several suggested answers or completions. Select the one that BEST answers the question or completes the statement. *PRINT THE LETTER OF THE CORRECT ANSWER IN THE SPACE AT THE RIGHT.*

Questions 1-25.

DIRECTIONS: Questions 1 through 25 describe situations which might occur in a correctional institution. The institution houses its inmates in cells divided into groups called cellblocks. In answering the questions, assume that you are a correction officer.

1. *Correction officers are often required to search inmates and the various areas of the correctional institution for any items which may be considered dangerous or which are not permitted. In making a routine search, officers should not neglect to examine an item just because it is usually regarded as a permitted item. For instance, some innocent-looking object can be converted into a weapon by sharpening one of its parts or replacing a part with a sharpened or pointed blade.* 1.____

   Which of the following objects could MOST easily be converted into a weapon in this way? A

   A. ballpoint pen
   B. pad of paper
   C. crayon
   D. handkerchief

2. *Only authorized employees are permitted to handle keys. Under no circumstances should an inmate be permitted to use door keys. When not in use, all keys are to be deposited with the security officer.* 2.____

   Which one of the following actions does NOT violate these regulations?

   A. A correction officer has given a trusted inmate the key to a supply room and sends the inmate to bring back a specific item from that room.
   B. A priest comes to make authorized visits to inmates. The correction officer is very busy, so he gives the priest the keys needed to reach certain groups of cells.
   C. An inmate has a pass to go to the library. A cellblock officer examines the pass, then unlocks the door and lets the inmate through.
   D. At the end of the day, a correction officer puts his keys in the pocket of his street clothes and takes them home with him.

3. *Decisions about handcuffing or restraining inmates are often up to the correction officers involved. However, an officer is legally responsible for exercising good judgment and for taking necessary precautions to prevent harm both to the inmate involved and to others.* 3.____

   In which one of the following situations is handcuffing or other physical restraint MOST likely to be needed?

A. An inmate seems to have lost control of his senses and is banging his fists repeatedly against the bars of his cell.
B. During the past two weeks, an inmate has deliberately tried to start three fights with other inmates.
C. An inmate claims to be sick and refuses to leave his cell for a scheduled meal.
D. During the night, an inmate begins to shout and sing, disturbing the sleep of other inmates.

4. *Some utensils that are ordinarily used in a kitchen can also serve as dangerous weapons – for instance, vegetable parers, meat saws, skewers, and icepicks. These should be classified as extremely hazardous.* 4.___

The MOST sensible way of solving the problems caused by the use of these utensils in a correctional institution is to

A. try to run the kitchen without using any of these utensils
B. provide careful supervision of inmates using such utensils in the kitchen
C. assign only trusted inmates to kitchen duty and let them use the tools without regular supervision
D. take no special precautions since inmates are not likely to think of using these commonplace utensils as weapons

5. *Inmates may try to conceal objects that can be used as weapons or as escape devices. Therefore, routine searches of cells or dormitories are necessary for safety and security.* 5.___

Of the following, it would probably be MOST effective to schedule routine searches to take place

A. on regular days and always at the same time of day
B. on regular days but at different times of day
C. at frequent but irregular intervals, always at the same time of day
D. at frequent but irregular intervals and at different times of day

6. *One of the purposes of conducting routine searches for forbidden items is to discourage inmates from acquiring such items in the first place. Inmates should soon come to realize that only possessors of these items have reason to fear or resent such searches.* 6.___

Inmates are MOST likely to come to this realization if

A. the searching officer leaves every inmate's possessions in a mess to make it clear that a search has taken place
B. the searching officer confiscates something from every cell, though he may later return most of the items
C. other inmates are not told when a forbidden item is found in an inmate's possession
D. all inmates know that possession of a forbidden item will result in punishment

7. Suppose you are a correction officer supervising a work detail of 22 inmates. All 22 checked in at the start of the work period. Making an informal count an hour later, you count only 21 inmates. 7.___
What is the FIRST action to take?

A. Count again to make absolutely sure how many inmates are present.
B. Report immediately that an inmate has escaped.
C. Try to figure out where the missing inmate could be.
D. Wait until the end of the work period and then make a formal roll call.

8. *The officer who is making a count at night when inmates are in bed must make sure he sees each man. The rule "see living breathing flesh" must be followed in making accurate counts.* 8.____

Of the following, which is the MOST likely reason for this rule?

A. An inmate may be concealing a weapon in the bed.
B. A bed may be arranged to give the appearance of being occupied even when the inmate is not there.
C. Waking inmates for the count is a good disciplinary measure because it shows them that they are under constant guard.
D. It is important for officers on duty at night to have something to do to keep them busy.

9. *When counting a group of inmates on a work assignment, great care should be taken to insure accuracy. The count method should be adapted to the number of inmates and to the type of location.* 9.____

Suppose that you are supervising 15 inmates working in a kitchen. Most of them are moving about constantly, carrying dishes and equipment from one place to another. In order to make an accurate count, which of the following methods would be MOST suitable under these circumstances?

A. Have the inmates *freeze* where they are whenever you call for a count, even though some of them may be carrying hot pans or heavy stacks of dishes.
B. Have the inmates stop their work and gather in one place whenever it is necessary to make a count.
C. Circulate among the inmates and make an approximate count while they are working.
D. Divide the group into sections according to type of work and assign one inmate in each group to give you the number for this section.

10. *Officers on duty at entrances must exercise the greatest care to prevent movement of unauthorized persons. At vehicle entrances, all vehicles must be inspected and a record kept of their arrival and departure.* 10.____

Assume that, as a correction officer, you have been assigned to duty at a vehicle entrance. Which of the following is probably the BEST method of preventing the movement of unauthorized persons in vehicles?

A. If passenger identifications are checked when vehicle enters, no check is necessary when the vehicle leaves.
B. Passenger identifications should be checked for all vehicles when vehicle enters and when it leaves.

C. Passenger identifications need not be checked when vehicle enters, but should always be checked when vehicle leaves.
D. Except for official vehicles, passenger identifications should be checked when vehicle enters and when it leaves.

11. In making a routine search of an inmate's cell, an officer finds various items. Although there is no immediate danger, he is not sure whether the inmate is permitted to have one of the items. 11.___
Of the following, the BEST action for the officer to take is to

A. confiscate the item immediately
B. give the inmate the benefit of the doubt, and let him keep the item
C. consult his rule book or his supervising officer to find out whether the inmate is permitted to have the item
D. leave the item in the inmate's cell, but plan to report him for an infraction of the rules

12. *It is almost certain that there will be occasional escape attempts or an occasional riot or disturbance that requires immediate emergency action. A well-developed emergency plan for dealing with these events includes not only planning for prevention and control and planning for action during the disturbance, but also planning steps that should be taken when the disturbance is over.* 12.___

When a disturbance is ended, which of the following steps should be taken FIRST?

A. Punishing the ringleaders.
B. Giving first aid to inmates or other persons who were injured.
C. Making an institutional count of all inmates.
D. Adopting further security rules to make sure such an incident does not occur again.

13. *It is often important to make notes about an occurrence that will require a written report or personal testimony.* 13.___

Assume that a correction officer has made the following notes for the warden of the institution about a certain occurrence: *10:45 A.M. March 16, 2007. Cellblock A. Robert Brown was attacked by another inmate and knocked to the floor. Brown's head hit the floor hard. He was knocked out. I reported a medical emergency. Dr. Thomas Nunez came and examined Brown. The doctor recommended that Brown be transferred to the infirmary for observation. Brown was taken to the infirmary at 11:15 A.M.*
Which of the following important items of information is MISSING or is INCOMPLETE in these notes? The

A. time that the incident occurred
B. place where the incident occurred
C. names of both inmates involved in the fight
D. name of the doctor who made the medical examination

14. A correction officer has made the following notes for the warden of his institution about an incident involving an infraction of the rules: *March 29, 2007. Cellblock B-4. Inmates involved were A. Whitman, T. Brach, M. Purlin, M. Verey. Whitman and Brach started the trouble around 7:30 P.M. I called for assistance. Officer Haley and Officer Blair responded. Officer Blair got cut, and blood started running down his face. The bleeding looked very bad. He was taken to the hospital and needed eight stitches.* 14.____
Which of the following items of information is MISSING or is INCOMPLETE in these notes?

A. The time and date of the incident
B. The place of the incident
C. Which inmates took part in the incident
D. What the inmates did that broke the rules

15. Your supervising officer has instructed you to follow a new system for handling inmate requests. It seems to you that the new system is not going to work very well and that inmates may resent it. 15.____
What should you do?

A. Continue handling requests the old way but do not let your supervising officer know you are doing this.
B. Continue using the old system until you have a chance to discuss the matter with your supervising officer.
C. Begin using the new system but plan to discuss the matter with your supervising officer if the system really does not work well.
D. Begin using the new system but make sure the inmates know that it is not your idea and you do not approve of it.

16. *Inmates who are prison-wise may know a good many tricks for putting something over. For instance, it is an officer's duty to stop fights among inmates. Therefore, inmates who want to distract the officer's attention from something that is going on in one place may arrange for a phony fight to take place some distance away.* 16.____

To avoid being taken in by a trick like this, a correction officer should

A. ignore any fights that break out among inmates
B. always make an inspection tour to see what is going on elsewhere before breaking up a fight
C. be alert for other suspicious activity when there is any disturbance
D. refuse to report inmates involved in a fight if the fight seems to have been phony

17. *Copies of the regulations are posted at various locations in the cellblock so that inmates can refer to them.* 17.____

Suppose that one of the regulations is changed and the correction officers receive revised copies to post in their cellblocks.
Of the following, the MOST effective way of informing the inmates of the revision is to

A. let the inmates know that you are taking down the old copies and putting up new ones in their place
B. post the new copies next to the old ones so that inmates will be able to compare them and learn about the change for themselves

C. leave the old copies up until you have had a chance to explain the change to each inmate
D. post the new copies in place of the old ones and also explain the change orally to the inmates

18. *A fracture is a broken bone. In a simple fracture, the skin is not broken. In a compound fracture, a broken end of the bone pierces the skin. Whenever a fracture is feared, the first thing to do is to prevent motion of the broken part.* 18.___

Suppose that an inmate has just tripped on a stairway and twisted his ankle. He says it hurts badly, but you cannot tell what is wrong merely by looking at it.
Of the following, the BEST action to take is to

A. tell the inmate to stand up and see whether he can walk
B. move the ankle gently to see whether you can feel any broken ends of bones
C. tell the inmate to rest a few minutes and promise to return later to see whether his condition has improved
D. tell the inmate not to move his foot and put in a call for medical assistance

19. *It is part of institutional procedure that at specified times during each 24-hour period all inmates in the institution are counted simultaneously. Each inmate must be counted at a specific place at a specified time. All movement of inmates ceases from the time the count starts until it is finished and cleared as correct.* 19.___

Assume that, as a correction officer, you are making such a count when an inmate in your area suddenly remembers he has an important 9 A.M. clinic appointment. You check his clinic pass and find that this is true.
What should you do?

A. Let him go to the clinic even though he may be counted again there.
B. Take him off your count and tell him to be sure he is included in the count being made at the clinic.
C. Keep him in your count and tell him to inform the officer at the clinic that he has already been counted.
D. Ask him to wait a few minutes until the counting period is over and then let him go to the clinic.

20. *Except in the case of a serious illness or injury (when a doctor should see the inmate immediately), emergency sick calls should be kept to a minimum, and inmates should be encouraged to wait for regular sick-call hours.* 20.___

In which of the following cases is an emergency sick call MOST likely to be justified? A(n)

A. inmate has had very severe stomach pains for several hours
B. inmate has cut his hand, and the bleeding has now stopped
C. inmate's glasses have been broken, and he is nearly blind without them
D. normally healthy inmate has lost his appetite and does not want to eat

21. *People who have lost their freedom are likely to go through periods of depression or to become extremely resentful or unpleasant. A correction officer can help inmates who are undergoing such periods of depression by respecting their feelings and treating them in a reasonable and tactful manner.* 21.____

Suppose that an inmate reacts violently to a single request made in a normal, routine manner by a correction officer. Of the following, which is likely to be the MOST effective way of handling the situation?

A. Point out to the inmate that it is his own fault that he is in jail, and he has nobody to blame for his troubles but himself.
B. Tell the inmate that he is acting childishly and that he had better straighten out.
C. Tell the inmate in a friendly way that you can see he is feeling down, but that he should comply with your request.
D. Let the inmate know that you are going to report his behavior unless he changes his attitude.

22. An inmate tells you, a correction officer, of his concern about the ability of his wife and children to pay for rent and food while he is in the institution. 22.____
Of the following, which is the BEST action to take?

A. Assure him that his wife and children are getting along fine, although you do not actually know this.
B. Put him in touch with the social worker or the correction employee who handles such problems.
C. Offer to lend him money yourself if his family is really in need.
D. Advise him to forget about his family and start concentrating on his own problems.

23. *It is particularly important to notice changes in the general pattern of an inmate's behavior. When an inmate who has been generally unpleasant and who has not spoken to an officer unless absolutely necessary becomes very friendly and cooperative, something has happened, and the officer should take steps to make sure what.* 23.____

Of the following possible explanations for this change in behavior, which one is the LEAST likely to be the real cause?

A. The inmate may be planning some kind of disturbance or escape attempt and is trying to fool the officer.
B. The inmate may be trying to get on the officer's good side for some reason of his own.
C. His friendliness and cooperation may indicate a developing mental illness.
D. He may be overcoming his initial hostile reactions to his imprisonment.

24. As a correction officer, you have an idea about a new way for handling a certain procedure. Your method would require a minor change in the regulations, but you are sure it would be a real improvement. 24.____
The BEST thing for you to do is to

A. discuss the idea with your supervising officer, explaining why it would work better than the present method
B. try your idea on your own cellblock, telling inmates that it is just an experiment and not official

C. attempt to get officers on other cellblocks to use your methods on a strictly unofficial basis
D. forget the whole thing since it might be too difficult to change the regulations

25. *Correction officers assigned to visiting areas have a dual supervisory function since their responsibilities include receiving persons other than inmates, as well as handling inmates. Here, of all places, it is important for an officer to realize that he is acting as a representative of his institution and that what he is doing is very much like public relations work.* 25.____

Assume that you are a correction officer assigned to duty in a visiting area.
Which of the following ways of carrying out this assignment is MOST likely to result in good public relations? You should

A. treat inmates and visitors sternly because this will let them know that the institution does not put up with any nonsense
B. be friendly to inmates but suspicious of visitors
C. be stern with inmates but polite and tactful with visitors
D. treat both inmates and visitors in a polite but tactful way

KEY (CORRECT ANSWERS)

1.	A	11.	C
2.	C	12.	B
3.	A	13.	C
4.	B	14.	D
5.	D	15.	C
6.	D	16.	C
7.	A	17.	D
8.	B	18.	D
9.	B	19.	D
10.	B	20.	A

21.	C
22.	B
23.	C
24.	A
25.	D

TEST 2

DIRECTIONS: Each question or incomplete statement is followed by several suggested answers or completions. Select the one that BEST answers the question or completes the statement. *PRINT THE LETTER OF THE CORRECT ANSWER IN THE SPACE AT THE RIGHT.*

Questions 1-5.

DIRECTIONS: Answer Questions 1 through 5 on the basis of the following passage.

The handling of supplies is an important part of correctional administration. A good deal of planning and organization is involved in purchase, stock control, and issue of bulk supplies to the cell-block. This planning is meaningless, however, if the final link in the chain – the cell-blook officer who is in charge of distributing supplies to the inmates – does not do his job in the proper way. First, when supplies are received, the officer himself should immediately check them or should personally supervise the checking, to make sure the count is correct. Nothing but trouble will result if an officer signs for 200 towels and discovers hours later that he is 20 towels short. Did the 20 towels "disappear," or did they never arrive in the first place? Second, all supplies should be locked up until they are actually distributed. Third, the officer must keep accurate records when supplies are issued. Complaints will be kept to a minimum if the officer makes sure that each inmate has received the supplies to which he is entitled, and if the officer can tell from his records when it is time to reorder to prevent a shortage. Fourth, the officer should either issue the supplies himself or else personally supervise the issuing. It is unfair and unwise to put an inmate in charge of supplies without giving him adequate supervision. A small thing like a bar of soap does not mean much to most people, but it means a great deal to the inmate who cannot even shave or wash up unless he receives the soap that is supposed to be issued to him.

1. Which one of the following jobs is NOT mentioned by the passage as the responsibility of a cellblock officer? 1.____

   A. Purchasing supplies
   B. Issuing supplies
   C. Counting supplies when they are delivered to the cellblock
   D. Keeping accurate records when supplies are issued

2. The passage says that supplies should be counted when they are delivered. Of the following, which is the BEST way of handling this job? 2.____

   A. The cellblock officer can wait until he has some free time and then count them himself.
   B. An inmate can start counting them right away, even if the cellblock officer cannot supervise his work.
   C. The cellblock officer can personally supervise an inmate who counts the supplies when they are delivered.
   D. Two inmates can count them when they are delivered, supervising each other's work.

3. The passage gives an example concerning a delivery of 200 towels that turned out to be 20 towels short. 3.___
The example is used to show that

   A. the missing towels were stolen
   B. the missing towels never arrived in the first place
   C. it is impossible to tell what happened to the missing towels because no count was made when they were delivered
   D. it does not matter that the missing towels were not accounted for because it is never possible to keep track of supplies accurately

4. The MAIN reason given by the passage for making a record when supplies are issued is that keeping records 4.___

   A. will discourage inmates from stealing supplies
   B. is a way of making sure that each inmate receives the supplies to which he is entitled
   C. will show the officer's superiors that he is doing his job in the proper way
   D. will enable the inmates to help themselves to any supplies they need

5. The passage says that it is unfair to put an inmate in charge of supplies without giving him adequate supervision. 5.___
Which of the following is the MOST likely explanation of why it would be *unfair* to do this?

   A. A privilege should not be given to one inmate unless it is given to all the other inmates too.
   B. It is wrong to make on inmate work when all the others can sit in their cells and do nothing.
   C. The cellblock officer should not be able to get out of doing a job by making an inmate do it for him.
   D. The inmate in charge of supplies could be put under pressure by other inmates to do them *special favors.*

Questions 6-10.

DIRECTIONS: Answer Questions 6 through 10 on the basis of the following passage.

The typical correction official must make predictions about the probable future behavior of his charges in order to make judgments affecting those individuals. In learning to predict behavior, the results of scientific studies of inmate behavior can be of some use. Most studies that have been made show that older men tend to obey rules and regulations better than younger men, and tend to be more reliable in carrying out assigned jobs. Men who had good employment records on the outside also tend to be more reliable than men whose records show haphazard employment or unemployment. Oddly enough, men convicted of crimes of violence are less likely to be troublemakers than men convicted of burglary or other crimes involving stealth. While it might be expected that first offenders would be much less likely to be troublemakers than men with previous convictions, the difference between the two groups is not very great. It must be emphasized, however, that predictions based on a man's background are only likelihoods – they are never certainties. A successful correction officer learns to give some weight to a man's background, but he should rely even more heavily on his own personal judgment of the individual in question. A good officer will develop in time a kind of sixth sense about human beings that is more reliable than any statistical predictions.

6. The passage suggests that knowledge of scientific studies of inmate behavior would PROBABLY help the correction officer to 6.____

   A. make judgments that affect the inmates in his charge
   B. write reports on all major infractions of the rules
   C. accurately analyze how an inmate's behavior is determined by his background
   D. change the personalities of the individuals in his charge

7. According to the information in the passage, which one of the following groups of inmates would tend to be MOST reliable in carrying out assigned jobs? 7.____

   A. Older men with haphazard employment records
   B. Older men with regular employment records
   C. Younger men with haphazard employment records
   D. Younger men with regular employment records

8. According to the information in the passage, which of the following are MOST likely to be troublemakers? 8.____

   A. Older men convicted of crimes of violence
   B. Younger men convicted of crimes of violence
   C. Younger men convicted of crimes involving stealth
   D. First offenders convicted of crimes of violence

9. The passage indicates that information about a man's background is 9.____

   A. a sure way of predicting his future behavior
   B. of no use at all in predicting his future behavior
   C. more useful in predicting behavior than a correction officer's expert judgment
   D. less reliable in predicting behavior than a correction officer's expert judgment

10. The passage names two groups of inmates whose behavior might be expected to be quite different, but who in fact behave only slightly differently.
    These two groups are 10.____

    A. older men and younger men
    B. first offenders and men with previous convictions
    C. men with good employment records and men with records of haphazard employment or unemployment
    D. men who obey the rules and men who do not

Questions 11-17.

DIRECTIONS: Questions 11 through 17 are based on the following pictures of objects found in Cells A, B, C, and D in a correctional institution.

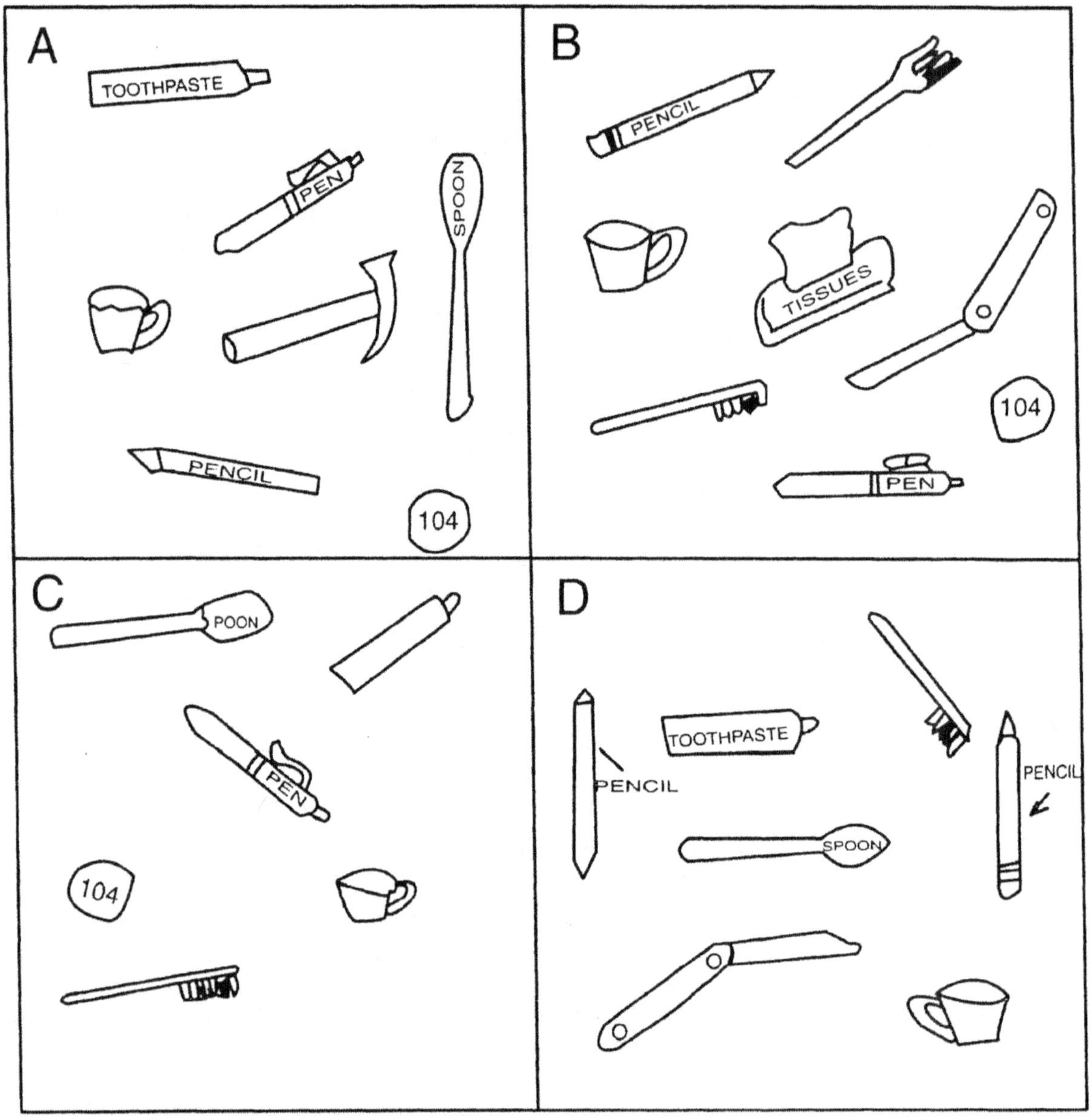

11. Which item can be found in every cell? 11.___

 A. Cup B. Money C. Pencil D. Toothpaste

12. Which cell has toothpaste but no toothbrush? 12.___

 A. A B. B C. C D. D

13. If knives and forks are prohibited in cells, how many cells are in violation of this rule? 13.___

 A. 1 B. 2 C. 3 D. 4

14. One inmate failed to return his tool in the woodworking shop before returning to his cell. That inmate is in Cell 14.___

 A. A B. B C. C D. D

15. The cell with the GREATEST number of objects is 15.____

A. A B. B C. C D. D

16. How many cells have AT LEAST one eating utensil? 16.____

A. 1 B. 2 C. 3 D. 4

17. Which cells contain money? 17.____

A. A, B, and C
B. A, B, and D
C. A, C, and D
D. B, C, and D

Questions 18-22.

DIRECTIONS: Answer Questions 18 through 22 on the basis of the following passage.

A large proportion of the people who are behind bars are not convicted criminals but people who have been arrested and are being held until their trial in court. Experts have often pointed out that this detention system does not operate fairly. For instance, a person who can afford to pay bail usually will not get looked up. The theory of the bail system is that the person will make sure to show up in court when he is supposed to since he knows that otherwise he will forfeit his bail -- he will lose the money he put up. Sometimes a person Who can show that he is a stable citizen with a job and a family will be released on "personal recognizance" (without bail). The result is that the well-to-do, the employed, and the family men can often avoid the detention system. The people who do wind up in detention tend to be the poor, the unemployed, the single, and the young.

18. According to the above passage, people who are put behind bars 18.____

A. are almost always dangerous criminals
B. include many innocent people who have been arrested by mistake
C. are often people who have been arrested but have not yet come to trial
D. are all poor people who tend to be young and single

19. The passage says that the detention system works *unfairly* against people who are 19.____

A. rich B. married C. old D. unemployed

20. The passage uses the expression *forfeit his bail.* Even if you have not seen the word *forfeit* before, you could figure out from the way it is used in the passage that *forfeiting* probably means ______ something. 20.____

A. losing track of
B. giving up
C. finding
D. avoiding

21. When someone is released on *personal recognizance,* this means that 21.____

A. the judge knows that he is innocent
B. he does not have to show up for a trial
C. he has a record of previous convictions
D. he does not have to pay bail

22. Suppose that two men were booked on the same charge at the same time, and that the same bail was set for both of them. One man was able to put up bail, and he was released. The second man was not able to put up bail, and he was held in detention. The reader of the passage would MOST likely feel that this result is 22.____

A. *unfair,* because it does not have any relation to guilt or innocence
B. *unfair,* because the first man deserves severe punishment
C. *fair,* because the first man is obviously innocent
D. *fair,* because the law should be tougher on poor people than on rich people

23. A certain cellblock has 240 inmates. From 8 A.M. to 9 A.M. on March 25, 120 inmates were assigned to cleanup work, and 25 inmates were sent for physical examinations. All the others remained in their cells. 23.____
How many inmates should have been in their cells during this hour?

A. 65 B. 85 C. 95 D. 105

24. There were 254 inmates in a certain cellblock at the beginning of the day. At 9:30 A.M., 12 inmates were checked out to the dispensary. At 10:00 A.M.,113 inmates were checked out to work details. At 10:30 A.M., 3 inmates were checked out to another cell-block. 24.____
How many inmates were present in this cellblock at 10:45 A.M. if none of the inmates who were checked out had returned?

A. 116 B. 126 C. 136 D. 226

25. There were 242 inmates in a certain cellblock at the beginning of the day. At 9:00 A.M., 116 inmates were checked out to a recreational program. At 9:15 A.M., 36 inmates were checked out to an educational program. At 9:30, 78 inmates were checked out on a work detail. By 10:15, the only inmates who had returned were 115 inmates who had been checked back in from the recreational program. A count made at 10:15 should show that the number of inmates present in the cellblock is 25.____

A. 127 B. 128 C. 135 D. 137

KEY (CORRECT ANSWERS)

1. A
2. C
3. C
4. B
5. D

6. A
7. B
8. C
9. D
10. B

11. A
12. A
13. B
14. A
15. B

16. D
17. A
18. C
19. D
20. B

21. D
22. A
23. C
24. B
25. A

EXAMINATION SECTION
TEST 1

DIRECTIONS: Each question or incomplete statement is followed by several suggested answers or completions. Select the one that BEST answers the question or completes the statement. *PRINT THE LETTER OF THE CORRECT ANSWER IN THE SPACE AT THE RIGHT.*

Questions 1-3.

DIRECTIONS: Questions 1 through 3 are based on the following example of a correction officer's report. The report consists of sixteen numbered sentences, some of which are not consistent with the principles of good report writing in correctional matters.

1. On January 5, I was assigned as the *A* officer on the third floor of Institution *Y* during the 12 midnight to 8 A.M. tour of duty. *2.* At about 1:30 A.M. on said date, I heard a cry for help coming from the lower *A* section of the floor. *3.* I immediately ran into the section and found inmate John Doe in cell number 5 holding up inmate Robert James who was hanging from the light fixture of the cell by a bedsheet. *4.* One end of the bedsheet was tied to the outer frame of the light fixture, and the other end was tied around the neck of inmate James. *5.* I immediately ran to the telephone to notify the control room for assistance. *6.* While waiting for assistance, I notified Correction Officer Harold Smith who was assigned as the *B* officer on the floor, and instructed inmate Doe to keep holding the hanging inmate in an upward position. *7.* Correction Officer Thomas Jones arrived at the scene together with Dr. Walter Frazer, who was the physician on duty in the institution at the time. *8.* Correction Officer Smith and I then ran to cell number 5, while Correction Officer Jones operated the *A* section locking mechanism to open the door to cell number 5. *9.* When the cell door was opened, I, together with Correction Officer Smith and Dr. Frazer, entered the cell where I cut the bedsheet with my pen knife to let the hanging inmate down. *10.* I found no suicide note in the cell. *11.* Dr. Frazer ordered the inmate to be placed on the floor outside of the cell so that he could inject emergency medication into the inmate's chest and administer artificial respiration. *12.* Both Correction Officer Smith and I assisted in administering artificial respiration under the physician's supervision. *13.* After the administration of artificial respiration for a period of approximately one-half hour, Dr. Frazer pronounced inmate James dead. *14.* The dead inmate's cell partner, inmate John Doe, stated that he awoke from his sleep and saw his cell partner hanging from the ceiling with a sheet tied around his neck. *15.* There were no pictures anywhere in the cell which would give information as to the deceased's family ties. *16.* It is believed that inmate James committed suicide because of his concern about the sentence he would receive when he appeared in court for sentencing on January 6.

1. A good report should be arranged in logical order. Which of the following sentences from the report does NOT appear in its proper sequence in the report? Sentence 1.____

   A. 2 B. 3 C. 10 D. 13

2. Only material that is relevant to the main thought of a report should be included. Which of the following sentences from the report contains material which is LEAST relevant to this report? Sentence 2.____

   A. 8 B. 11 C. 14 D. 15

3. Good reports should contain accurate statements based upon definite information. Which of the following sentences from the report contains material which is NOT based on definite information? 3.___
Sentence

A. 5 B. 6 C. 9 D. 16

4. Failure to choose words in written reports that exactly express the thought the writer has in mind results in many a minor mystery for the reader. 4.___
Of the following, the MOST important idea in this statement is that

A. good reports do not contain ambiguous statements
B. poor report writers do not have sufficient experience for clear writing
C. some individuals are poor readers and cannot comprehend even the most simple report
D. good reports do not contain difficult words

5. Unless a report writer uses care, he cannot effectively communicate his thoughts to those receiving and reading his report. Clear thinking must precede clear writing. In accordance with this statement, it is good practice for report writers to 5.___

A. write the report quickly before the details are forgotten
B. use concrete words to communicate effectively
C. plan the report before writing it
D. prepare the report with as many facts as possible

Questions 6-8.

DIRECTIONS: Questions 6 through 8 contain two statements. Each statement may contain one or more sentences. Choose answer
A. if both statements are correct
B. if neither statement is correct
C. if statement I only is correct but not statement II
D. if statement II only is correct but not statement I

6. I. There is a definite relationship between the length of a report and its clarity. Many report writers who have difficulty conveying their ideas clearly to their readers find upon examination that their reports are very long and that the reader is confused because the ideas are hidden in a profusion of words. 6.___
II. Good report writers know that deciding what to leave out is almost as important as deciding what goes into their report. Words, ideas, or facts that are not essential to the understanding or acceptance of their reports can only obscure and weaken them.

7. I. An extensive vocabulary is a fine asset. It enables you to grasp quickly the ideas tossed at you and it may help you to put your ideas across to someone with a smaller or different stock of words because he will eventually come to understand your style of writing. 7.___
II. It is seldom necessary to make an outline for your written report because the statement of witnesses and other individuals involved in the subject matter of your report provides sufficient data.

8\. I. The need to write with an air of professionalism does not make the job of a report writer any easier or more secure because it gives the indication of a pedantic person who is only interested in creating an impression. 8.____

II. The conclusion of a written report should contain the writer's evaluation or opinion of the occurrence and any suggestions or recommendations with reference to the incident.

Questions 9-13.

DIRECTIONS: Questions 9 through 13 consist of passages of two or more sentences. Each of the passages contains an incorrectly used word. First decide which is the incorrectly used word. Then, from among the options given, decide which word, when substituted for the incorrectly used word, makes the meaning of the passage clear.

<u>Study the following example</u>:

Like the monastery, mental hospital, school youth camp, and military base, the correctional institution is a people-changing organization. All these organizations work with concrete material.

A. human B. criminal C. woven D. religious

The word *concrete* in the passage does not convey the meaning the passage is evidently intended to convey - that all these organizations share a common characteristic, their work with people. Choices B and D do not apply to ALL the organizations listed. Choice C has no relation to the paragraph. Only choice A (*human*), when substituted for the word *concrete,* makes the meaning of the passage clear.
Accordingly, the answer to the question is A.

9\. The prison qualifies as a bureaucracy because it has administrative impediments established to maintain its organization, a hierarchy of authority among its employees, and a system of enforcement for its rules. 9.____

A. inmates B. machinery C. purchases D. democracy

10\. In a situation where inmates have minimal recourse to staff, they are also more vulnerable to abuse and exploitation by other inmates. As a consequence, inmates tend to become progressively more trusting of each other as well as of staff. 10.____

A. wary
B. conspicuous
C. compliant
D. contrary

11\. Obviously no institution can be operated safely and efficiently unless its occupants conform to some standards of improper behavior. Furthermore, a requirement that inmates be peaceable and industrious can be justified as preparing them for a law-abiding life in the free community. 11.____

A. resentful
B. orderly
C. unconcerned
D. difficult

12. Caseloads of different types of offenders should vary in size and in type and intensity of mitigation. Classification and assignment of offenders should be made according to their needs and problems. 12.___

A. treatment
B. approximation
C. population
D. emancipation

13. Strong and informed administrative support in State correctional programs will be required to upgrade services and to adopt the practices of private industry. Labor organizations and business firms could be of inestimable help in advising and digressing the development of new programs, and in neutralizing opposition to them. 13.___

A. grafting
B. guiding
C. prohibiting
D. consuming

Questions 14-15.

DIRECTIONS: Answer Questions 14 and 15 SOLELY on the basis of the following passage. The public has become increasingly aware that rehabilitation–that great battle cry of prison reform – is one of the great myths of 20th-century penology. The hard truth is that punishment and retribution are the primary, if not the only, functions served by most correctional institutions. Courts can provide enlightened rule-making to assist prison reform and ombudsmen can give prisoners a forum to consider their complaints but the results would be limited. The corrections system will never run with any real efficiency until: (a) prisoners want to be reformed; (b) prison administrators want to help them reform; (c) courts want to help both toward a system of reform; and (d) they all define reform in the same way. If this is not done, the criminal justice system will continue to operate on the model of concentric layers of coercion, a grossly inefficient model.

14. According to the above selection, all of the following will be required in order to improve the corrections system EXCEPT 14.___

A. commitment to reform by prison administrators
B. development by penal experts of criteria for meaningful rehabilitation
C. acceptance by prisoners of the need for their cooperation
D. assistance by the courts in providing a system where reform is possible

15. According to the above selection, meaningful prison reform is MOST likely to result from 15.___

A. the appointment of ombudsmen to replace the courts in ruling on prisoners' complaints
B. coordination by sociologists of efforts to improve prison conditions
C. a realization by society that rehabilitation of prisoners is no longer a realistic objective
D. the joint efforts of those directly concerned and a common understanding of the goals to be achieved

Questions 16-19.

DIRECTIONS: Questions 16 through 19 are to be answered SOLELY on the basis of the following passage.

Morally, there is no basis for the assertion that the commission of a social offense allows society to strip a human being of all his rights except those which, through some sort of *natural law* concept, he needs to survive. Rather, society is justified in punishing offenders only to the extent that it needs to protect itself; excessive retribution is *immoral.* Thus, unless society can demonstrate that a specific deprivation is necessary to its self-preservation, or to its reassertion of authority over the individual offender, it should not be entitled to enforce the deprivation. To place the burden on the prisoner to demonstrate that he should not be deprived of a particular right appears to be unfair and unjustified for two reasons: (1) the resources and skills are unequally distributed in society's favor; (2) the concept of *proportionality* as a rudimentary value is rejected by such an approach, which even theories of retribution and vengeance do not support.

Pragmatically, too, prisoners should be viewed and treated as human beings. Ninety-five percent of all those incarcerated in prisons are returned to the free world. It violates common sense to expect a man who has been treated at best as a cipher while in prison to be enamored of a society which has not only enchained him but also has increased his torment while he is confined. When he is released, his action is likely to be antisocial rather than social. Additionally, the imposition of excessive suffering on offenders permeates society's attitudes toward others in its midst. Just as we are now realizing that violence abroad erodes the barriers against domestic violence, official hostility toward some human beings tends to add an aura of authority to hostility toward and among others. Disinclination to cherish humanity at one point in society leads to total abdication of humanity at another.

16. In the above passage, it is pointed out that 16.____

    A. it is a practical approach to treatment to take away all but the basic rights of a prisoner
    B. it is proper to remove an inmate's rights within a system of rewards and punishments
    C. incarceration should not be used for revenge against one who has offended society
    D. the inmate ought to play a primary role in determining treatment methods

17. According to the above passage, 17.____

    A. inmates who are treated badly are apt to resort to antisocial behavior when they are returned to society
    B. there is a tendency among inmates to join organizations dedicated to achieving civil rights for the victims of society
    C. society generally sees all inmates as being equal despite inconsistent observation of prisoners' rights
    D. recidivism is a serious problem for the majority of prisoners who are released on parole

18. While criticizing the kind of treatment prisoners receive in our institutions, the passage implies that 18.____

    A. the mistreatment of prisoners is an outcome of society's benign attitude toward the law-abiding citizen
    B. cruelty begets cruelty, and that humane treatment will make better citizens of those entrusted to our care
    C. when violence in this country spreads, it increases all over the world
    D. an aura of authority has replaced official hostility in correctional institutions

19. According to the above passage, penal authorities are justified in depriving prisoners of rights 19.___

A. in order to satisfy society's desire for retribution against criminal offenders
B. until prisoners can demonstrate that particular deprivations are unjustified
C. whenever the preservation of order within the institution will be facilitated
D. only when it is necessary to protect society or maintain control over the inmate

Questions 20-25.

DIRECTIONS: Questions 20 through 25 are to be answered on the basis of the following notes and tables.

1. Assume that a certain imaginary jurisdiction, Perryville, contains five correctional institutions. These facilities are named Howe, Jackson, Grant, Pershing, and Marshall.
2. Assume that there are 365 days in each year.
3. Assume that the number of inmates at each institution listed above does not change during 1995 or 2000.

TABLE A

Some Characteristics of
Perryville's Correctional Facilities - 1995

Facility	Inmate Population (No. of Inmates)	Yearly Budget	Daily Cost Per Inmate	Total Personnel (staff)	Ratio of Staff to Inmate Population
Howe	75	$1,916,250	$70.00	25	1:3
Jackson	100	$1,825,000		25	1:4
Grant	125	$2,007,500	$44.00	25	1:5
Pershing		$2,427,250	$35.00		1:5
Marshall	375		$52.50	125	1:3

TABLE B

Some Characteristics of
Perryville's Correctional Facilities - 2000

Facility	Inmate Population (No. of Inmates)	Yearly Budget	Daily Cost Per Inmate	Total Personnel (staff)	Ratio of Staff to Inmate Population
Howe	90	$2,299,500	$70.00	30	1:3
Jackson	140	$2,810,500	$55.00	20	1:7
Grant	150	$2,737,500	$50.00	25	1:6
Pershing	200	$2,920,000	$40.00	50	1:4
Marshall	300	$6,022,500	$55.00	60	1:5

20. In 1995, the daily cost per inmate at the Jackson Correctional Facility was 20.___

A. $41.00 B. $50.00 C. $62.50 D. $65.00

21. If the total number of inmates at all five of Perryville's correctional institutions was 865 in 1995, the total number of personnel at the Pershing Correctional Institution during the same year was 21.____

A. 28 B. 32 C. 36 D. 38

22. In 2000, the percentage of the total inmate population of Perryville's correctional facilities held at the Grant Facility was MOST NEARLY 22.____

A. 14% B. 17% C. 23% D. 32%

23. The average number of personnel at Perryville's correctional institutions in 2000 was MOST NEARLY 23.____

A. 28 B. 38 C. 47 D. 168

24. Of the following, the facility which showed the greatest percent increase in number of inmates in 2000 as compared to 1995 was 24.____

A. Marshall B. Grant C. Jackson D. Howe

25. If, for 2001, the total inmate population of Perryville's five correctional institutions increased by 200 inmates, the percentage increase over the total 2000 population was MOST NEARLY 25.____

A. 18% B. 23% C. 31% D. 33%

KEY (CORRECT ANSWERS)

1. C
2. D
3. D
4. A
5. C
6. A
7. B
8. D
9. B
10. A
11. B
12. A
13. B
14. B
15. D
16. C
17. A
18. B
19. D
20. B
21. D
22. B
23. B
24. C
25. B

EXAMINATION SECTION
TEST 1

DIRECTIONS: Each question or incomplete statement is followed by several suggested answers or completions. Select the one that BEST answers the question or completes the statement. *PRINT THE LETTER OF THE CORRECT ANSWER IN THE SPACE AT THE RIGHT.*

1. Of the following, the MOST important single factor in any building security program is 1.____

   A. a fool-proof employee identification system
   B. an effective control of entrances and exits
   C. bright illumination of all outside areas
   D. clearly marking public and non-public areas

2. There is general agreement that the BEST criterion of what is a good physical security system in a large public building is 2.____

   A. the number of uniformed officers needed to patrol sensitive areas
   B. how successfully the system prevents rather than detects violations
   C. the number of persons caught in the act of committing criminal offenses
   D. how successfully the system succeeds in maintaining good public relations

3. Which one of the following statements most correctly expresses the CHIEF reason why women were originally made eligible for appointment to the position of officer? 3.____

   A. Certain tasks in security protection can be performed best by assigning women.
   B. More women than men are available to fill many vacancies in this position.
   C. The government wants more women in law enforcement because of their better attendance records.
   D. Women can no longer be barred from any government jobs because of sex.

4. The MOST BASIC purpose of patrol by officers is to 4.____

   A. eliminate as much as possible the opportunity for successful misconduct
   B. investigate criminal complaints and accident cases
   C. give prompt assistance to employees and citizens in distress or requesting their help
   D. take persons into custody who commit criminal offenses against persons and property

5. The highest quality of patrol service is MOST generally obtained by 5.____

   A. frequently changing the post assignments of each officer
   B. assigning officers to posts of equal size
   C. assigning problem officers to the least desirable posts
   D. assigning the same officers to the same posts

6. The one of the following requirements which is MOST essential to the successful performance of patrol duty by individual officers is their 6.____

   A. ability to communicate effectively with higher-level officers
   B. prompt signalling according to a prescribed schedule to insure post coverages at all times

C. knowledge of post conditions and post hazards
D. willingness to cover large areas during periods of critical manpower shortages

7. Officers on patrol are constantly warned to be on the alert for suspicious persons, actions, and circumstances. 7.____
With this in mind, a senior officer should emphasize the need for them to

A. be cautious and suspicious when dealing officially with any civilian regardless of the latter's overt actions or the circumstances surrounding his dealings with the police
B. keep looking for the unusual persons, actions, and circumstances on their posts and pay less attention to the usual
C. take aggressive police action immediately against any unusual person or condition detected on their posts, regardless of any other circumstances
D. become thoroughly familiar with the usual on their posts so as to be better able to detect the unusual

8. Of primary importance in the safeguarding of property from theft is a good central lock and key issuance and control system. 8.____
Which one of the following recommendations about maintaining such a control system would be LEAST acceptable?

A. In selecting locks to be used for the various gates, building, and storage areas, consideration should be given to the amount of security desired.
B. Master keys should have no markings that will identify them as such and the list of holders of these keys should be frequently reviewed to determine the continuing necessity for the individuals having them.
C. Whenever keys for outside doors or gates or for other doors which permit access to important buildings and areas are misplaced, the locks should be immediately changed or replaced pending an investigation.
D. Whenever an employee fails to return a borrowed key at the time specified, a prompt investigation should be made by the security force.

9. In a crowded building, a fire develops in the basement, and smoke enters the crowded rooms on the first floor. Of the following, the BEST action for an officer to take after an alarm is turned in is to 9.____

A. call out a warning that the building is on fire and that everyone should evacuate because of the immediate danger
B. call all of the officers together for an emergency meeting and discuss a plan of action
C. immediately call for assistance from the local police station to help in evacuating the crowd
D. tell everyone that there is a fire in the building next door and that they should move out onto the streets through available exits

10. Which of the following is in a key position to carry out successfully a safety program of an agency? The 10.____

A. building engineer
B. bureau chiefs
C. immediate supervisors
D. public relations director

11. It is GENERALLY considered that a daily roll call inspection, which checks to see that the officers and their equipment are in good order, is 11.____

A. *desirable,* chiefly because it informs the superior officer what men will have to purchase new uniforms within a month
B. *desirable,* chiefly because the public forms their impressions of the organization from the appearance of the officers
C. *undesirable,* chiefly because this kind of daily inspection unnecessarily delays officers in getting to their assigned patrol posts
D. *undesirable,* chiefly because roll call inspection usually misses individuals reporting to work late

12. A supervising officer in giving instructions to a group of officers on the principles of accident investigation remarked, "A conclusion that appears reasonable will often be changed by exploring a factor of apparently little importance". 12.____
Which one of the following precautions does this statement emphasize as MOST important in any accident investigation?

A. Every accident clue should be fully investigated.
B. Accidents should not be too promptly investigated.
C. Only specially trained officers should investigate accidents.
D. Conclusions about accident causes are highly unreliable.

13. On a rainy day, a senior officer found that 9 of his 50 officers reported to work. 13.____
What percentage of his officers was ABSENT?

A. 18% B. 80% C. 82% D. 90%

14. Officer A and Officer B work at the same post on the same days, but their hours are different. Officer A comes to work at 9:00 A.M. and leaves at 5:00 P.M., with a lunch period between 12:15 P.M. and 1:15 P.M. Officer B comes to work at 10:50 A.M. and works until 6:50 P.M., and he takes an hour for lunch between 3:00 P.M. and 4:00 P.M. What is the total amount of time between 9:00 A.M. and 6:50 P.M. that only ONE officer will be on duty? 14.____

A. 4 hours
B. 4 hours and 40 minutes
C. 5 hours
D. 5 hours and 40 minutes

15. An officer's log recorded the following attendance of 30 officers: 15.____

Monday	20	present;	10	absent
Tuesday	28	present;	2	absent
Wednesday	30	present;	0	absent
Thursday	21	present;	9	absent
Friday	16	present;	14	absent
Saturday	11	present;	19	absent
Sunday	14	present;	16	absent

On the average, how many men were present on the weekdays (Monday - Friday)?

A. 21 B. 23 C. 25 D. 27

16. An angry woman is being questioned by an officer when she begins shouting abuses at him. 16.____
The BEST of the following procedures for the officer to follow is to

A. leave the room until she has cooled off
B. politely ignore anything she says
C. place her under arrest by handcuffing her to a fixed object
D. warn her that he will have to use force to restrain her making remarks

17. Of the following, which is NOT a recommended practice for an officer placing a woman offender under arrest? 17.____

A. Assume that the offender is an innocent and virtuous person and treat her accordingly.
B. Protect himself from attack by the woman.
C. Refrain from using excessive physical force on the offender.
D. Make the public aware that he is not abusing the woman.

Questions 18-21.

DIRECTIONS: Questions 18 through 21 are to be answered SOLELY on the basis of the following passage.

Specific measures for prevention of pilferage will be based on careful analysis of the conditions at each agency. The most practical and effective method to control casual pilferage is the establishment of psychological deterrents.

One of the most common means of discouraging casual pilferage is to search individuals leaving the agency at unannounced times and places. These spot searches may occasionally detect attempts at theft but greater value is realized by bringing to the attention of individuals the fact that they may be apprehended if they do attempt the illegal removal of property.

An aggressive security education program is an effective means of convincing employees that they have much more to lose than they do to gain by engaging in acts of theft. It is important for all employees to realize that pilferage is morally wrong no matter how insignificant the value of the item which is taken. In establishing any deterrent to casual pilferage, security officers must not lose sight of the fact that most employees are honest and disapprove of thievery. Mutual respect between security personnel and other employees of the agency must be maintained if the facility is to be protected from other more dangerous forms of human hazards. Any security measure which infringes on the human rights or dignity of others will jeopardize, rather than enhance, the overall protection of the agency.

18. The $100,000 yearly inventory of an agency revealed that $50 worth of goods had been stolen; the only individuals with access to the stolen materials were the employees. Of the following measures, which would the author of the preceding paragraph MOST likely recommend to a security officer? 18.____

A. Conduct an intensive investigation of all employees to find the culprit.
B. Make a record of the theft, but take no investigative or disciplinary action against any employee.
C. Place a tight security check on all future movements of personnel.
D. Remove the remainder of the material to an area with much greater security.

19. What does the passage imply is the percentage of employees whom a security officer should expect to be honest? 19.____

A. No employee can be expected to be honest all of the time
B. Just 50%
C. Less than 50%
D. More than 50%

20. According to the passage, the security officer would use which of the following methods to minimize theft in buildings with many exits when his staff is very small? 20.____

A. Conduct an inventory of all material and place a guard near that which is most likely to be pilfered.
B. Inform employees of the consequences of legal prosecution for pilfering.
C. Close off the unimportant exits and have all his men concentrate on a few exits.
D. Place a guard at each exit and conduct a casual search of individuals leaving the premises.

21. Of the following, the title BEST suited for this passage is: 21.____

A. Control Measures for Casual Pilfering
B. Detecting the Potential Pilferer
C. Financial losses Resulting from Pilfering
D. The Use of Moral Persuasion in Physical Security

22. Of the following first aid procedures, which will cause the GREATEST harm in treating a fracture? 22.____

A. Control hemorrhages by applying direct pressure
B. Keep the broken portion from moving about
C. Reset a protruding bone by pressing it back into place
D. Treat the suffering person for shock

23. During a snowstorm, a man comes to you complaining of frostbitten hands. PROPER first aid treatment in this case is to 23.____

A. place the hands under hot running water
B. place the hands in lukewarm water
C. call a hospital and wait for medical aid
D. rub the hands in melting snow

24. While on duty, an officer sees a woman apparently in a state of shock. Of the following, which one is NOT a symptom of shock? 24.____

A. Eyes lacking luster
B. A cold, moist forehead
C. A shallow, irregular breathing
D. A strong, throbbing pulse

25. You notice a man entering your building who begins coughing violently, has shortness of breath, and complains of severe chest pains. These symptoms are GENERALLY indicative of 25.____

A. a heart attack
B. a stroke
C. internal bleeding
D. an epileptic seizure

26. When an officer is required to record the rolled fingerprint impressions of a prisoner on the standard fingerprint form, the technique recommended by the F.B.I, as MOST likely to result in obtaining clear impressions is to roll 26.____

A. all fingers away from the center of the prisoner's body
B. all fingers toward the center of the prisoner's body
C. the thumbs away from and the other fingers toward the center of the prisoner's body
D. the thumbs toward and the other fingers away from the center of the prisoner's body

27. The principle which underlies the operation and use of a lie detector machine is that 27.____

A. a person who is not telling the truth will be able to give a consistent story
B. a guilty mind will unconsciously associate ideas in a very indicative manner
C. the presence of emotional stress in a person will result in certain abnormal physical reactions
D. many individuals are not afraid to lie

Questions 28-32.

DIRECTIONS: Questions 28 through 32 are based SOLELY on the following diagram and the paragraph preceding this group of questions. The paragraph will be divided into two statements. Statement one (1) consists of information given to the senior officer by an agency director; *this information will detail the specific security objectives the senior officer has to meet.* Statement two (2) gives the resources available to the senior officer.

NOTE: The questions are correctly answered only when all of the agency's objectives have been met and when the officer has used all his resources efficiently (i.e., to their maximum effectiveness) in meeting these objectives. All X's in the diagram indicate possible locations of officers' posts. Each X has a corresponding number which is to be used when referring to that location.

DIAGRAM

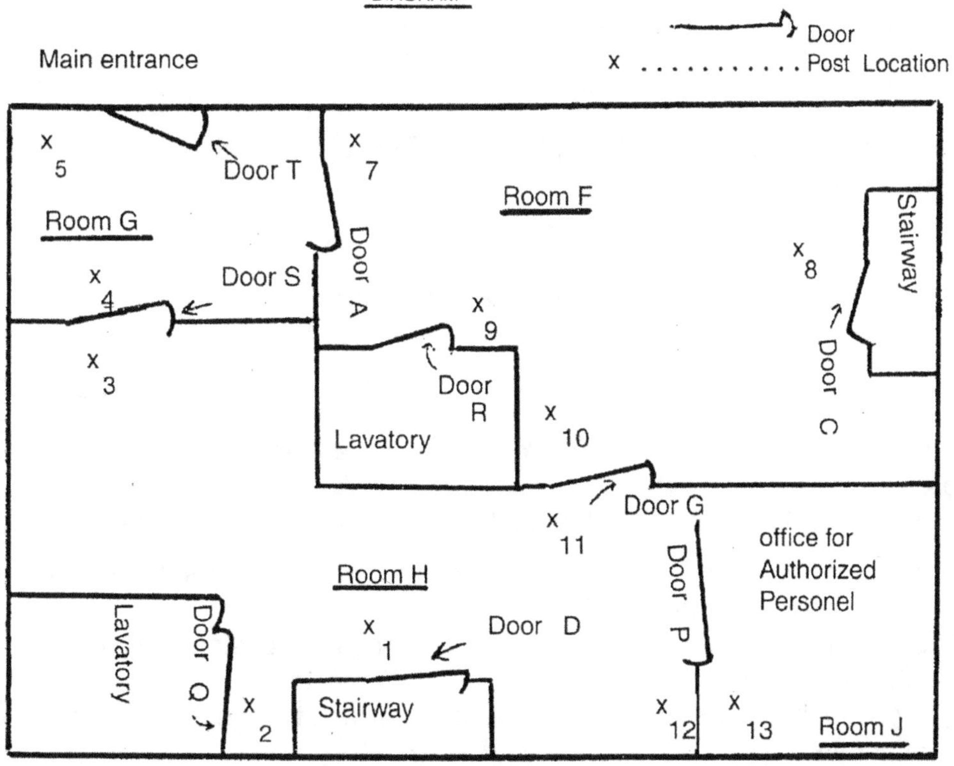

PARAGRAPH

PARAGRAPH

STATEMENT 1: Room G will be the public intake room from which persons will be directed to Room F or Room H; under no circumstances are they to enter the wrong room, and they are not to move from Room F to Room H or vice-versa. A minimum of two officers must be in each room frequented by the public at all times, and they are to keep unauthorized individuals from going to the second floor or into restricted areas. All usable entrances or exits must be covered.

STATEMENT 2: The senior officer can lock any door except the main entrance and stairway doors. He has a staff of five officers to carry out these operations.

NOTE: The senior officer is available for guard duty. Room J is an active office.

28. According to the instructions, how many officers should be assigned inside the office for authorized personnel (Room J)? 28.____

A. 0 B. 1 C. 2 D. 3

29. In order to keep the public from moving between Room F and Room H, which door(s) can be locked without interfering with normal office operations? Door 29.____

A. G B. P C. R and Q D. S

30. When placing officers in Room H, the only way the senior officer can satisfy the agency's objectives and his manpower limitations is by placing men at locations 30.___

A. 1 and 3 B. 1 and 12 C. 3 and 11 D. 11 and 12

31. In accordance with the instructions, the LEAST effective locations to place officers in Room F are locations 31.___

A. 7 and 9 B. 7 and 10 C. 8 and 9 D. 9 and 10

32. In which room is it MOST difficult for each of the officers to see all the movements of the public? Room 32.___

A. G B. F C. H D. J

33. According to its own provisions, the Penal Law of the State has a number of general purposes. 33.___
It would be LEAST accurate to state that one of these general purposes is to

A. give fair warning of the nature of the conduct forbidden and the penalties authorized upon conviction
B. define the act or omission and accompanying mental state which constitute each offense
C. regulate the procedure which governs the arrest, trial and punishment of convicted offenders
D. insure the public safety by preventing the commission of offenses through the deterrent influence of the sentences authorized upon conviction

34. Officers must be well-informed about the meaning of certain terms in connection with their enforcement duties. Which one of the following statements about such terms would be MOST accurate according to the Penal Law of the State? A(n) 34.___

A. offense is always a crime
B. offense is always a violation
C. violation is never a crime
D. felony is never an offense

35. According to the Penal Law of the State, the one of the following elements which must ALWAYS be present in order to justify the arrest of a person for criminal assault is 35.___

A. the infliction of an actual physical injury
B. an intent to cause an injury
C. a threat to inflict a physical injury
D. the use of some kind of weapon

36. A recent law of the State defines who are police officers and who are peace officers. The official title of this law is: The 36.___

A. Criminal Code of Procedure
B. Law of Criminal Procedure
C. Criminal Procedure Law
D. Code of Criminal Procedure

37. If you are required to appear in court to testify as the complainant in a criminal action, it would be MOST important for you to 37.____

A. confine your answers to the questions asked when you are testifying
B. help the prosecutor even if some exaggeration in your testimony may be necessary
C. be as fair as possible to the defendant even if some details have to be omitted from your testimony
D. avoid contradicting other witnesses testifying against the defendant

38. A senior officer is asked by the television news media to explain to the public what happened on his post during an important incident. 38.____
When speaking with departmental permission in front of the tape recorders and cameras, the senior officer can give the MOST favorable impression of himself and his department by

A. refusing to answer any questions but remaining calm in front of the cameras
B. giving a detailed report of the wrong decisions made by his agency for handling the particular incident
C. presenting the appropriate factual information in a competent way
D. telling what should have been done during the incident and how such incidents will be handled in the future

39. Of the following suggested guidelines for officers, the one which is LEAST likely to be effective in promoting good manners and courtesy in their daily contacts with the public is: 39.____

A. Treat inquiries by telephone in the same manner as those made in person
B. Never look into the face of the person to whom you are speaking
C. Never give misinformation in answer to any inquiry on a matter on which you are uncertain of the facts
D. Show respect and consideration in both trivial and important contacts with the public

40. Assume you are an officer who has had a record of submitting late weekly reports and that you are given an order by your supervisor which is addressed to all line officers. The order states that weekly reports will be replaced by twice-weekly reports. 40.____
The MOST logical conclusion for you to make, of the following, is:

A. Fully detailed information was missing from your past reports
B. Most officers have submitted late reports
C. The supervisor needs more timely information
D. The supervisor is attempting to punish you for your past late reports

41. A young man with long hair and "mod" clothing makes a complaint to an officer about the rudeness of another officer. 41.____
If the senior officer is not on the premises, the officer receiving the complaint should

A. consult with the officer who is being accused to see if the youth's story is true
B. refer the young man to central headquarters
C. record the complaint made against his fellow officer and ask the youth to wait until he can locate the senior officer
D. search for the senior officer and bring him back to the site of the complainant

42. During a demonstration, which area should ALWAYS be kept clear of demonstrators? 42.____

A. Water fountains
B. Seating areas
C. Doorways
D. Restrooms

43. During demonstrations, an officer's MOST important duty is to 43.____

A. aid the agency's employees to perform their duties
B. promptly arrest those who might cause incidents
C. promptly disperse the crowds of demonstrators
D. keep the demonstrators from disrupting order

44. Of the following, what is the FIRST action a senior officer should take if a demonstration develops in his area without advance warning? 44.____

A. Call for additional assistance from the police department
B. Find the leaders of the demonstrators and discuss their demands
C. See if the demonstrators intend to break the law
D. Inform his superiors of the event taking place

45. If a senior officer is informed in the morning that a demonstration will take place during the afternoon at his assigned location, he should assemble his officers to discuss the nature and aspects of this demonstration. Of the following, the subject which it is LEAST important to discuss during this meeting is 45.____

A. making a good impression if an officer is called before the television cameras for a personal interview
B. the known facts and causes of the demonstration
C. the attitude and expected behavior of the demonstrators
D. the individual responsibilities of the officers during the demonstration

46. A male officer has probable reason to believe that a group of women occupying the ladies' toilet are using illicit drugs.
The BEST action, of the following, for the officer to take is to 46.____

A. call for assistance and, with the aid of such assistance, enter the toilet and escort the occupants outside
B. ignore the situation but recommend that the ladies' toilet be closed temporarily
C. immediately rush into the ladies' toilet and search the occupants therein
D. knock on the door of the ladies' toilet and ask their permission to enter so that he will not be accused of trying to molest them

47. Assume that you know that a group of demonstrators will not cooperate with your request to throw handbills in a waste basket instead of on the sidewalk. You ask one of the leaders of the group, who agrees with you, to speak to the demonstrators and ask for their cooperation in this matter.
Your request of the group leader is 47.____

A. *desirable,* chiefly because an officer needs civilians to control the public since the officer is usually unfriendly to the views of public groups
B. *undesirable,* chiefly because an officer should never request a civilian to perform his duties
C. *desirable,* chiefly because the appeal of an acknowledged leader helps in gaining group cooperation

D. *undesirable,* chiefly because an institutional leader is motivated to maneuver a situation to gain his own personal advantage

48. A vague letter received from a female employee in the agency accuses an officer of improper conduct. 48.____
The initial investigative interview by the senior officer assigned to check the accusation should GENERALLY be with the

A. accused officer
B. female employee
C. highest superior about disciplinary action against the officer
D. immediate supervisor of the female employee

Questions 49-50.

DIRECTIONS: Questions 49 and 50 are to be answered SOLELY on the basis of the information in the following paragraph.

The personal conduct of each member of the Department is the primary factor in promoting desirable police-community relations. Tact, patience, and courtesy shall be strictly observed under all circumstances. A favorable public attitude toward the police must be earned; it is influenced by the personal conduct and attitude of each member of the force, by his personal integrity and courteous manner, by his respect for due process of law, by his devotion to the principles of justice, fairness, and impartiality.

49. According to the preceding paragraph, what is the BEST action an officer can take in dealing with people in a neighborhood? 49.____

A. Assist neighborhood residents by doing favors for them.
B. Give special attention to the community leaders in order to be able to control them effectively.
C. Behave in an appropriate manner and give all community members the same just treatment.
D. Prepare a plan detailing what he, the officer, wants to do for the community and submit it for approval.

50. As used in the paragraph, the word *impartiality* means *most nearly* 50.____

A. observant
B. unbiased
C. righteousness
D. honesty

KEY (CORRECT ANSWERS)

1.	B	11.	B	21.	A	31.	D	41.	C
2.	B	12.	A	22.	C	32.	C	42.	C
3.	A	13.	C	23.	B	33.	C	43.	D
4.	A	14.	D	24.	D	34.	C	44.	D
5.	D	15.	B	25.	A	35.	A	45.	A
6.	C	16.	B	26.	D	36.	C	46.	A
7.	D	17.	A	27.	C	37.	A	47.	C
8.	C	18.	B	28.	A	38.	C	48.	B
9.	D	19.	D	29.	A	39.	B	49.	C
10.	C	20.	B	30.	B	40.	C	50.	B

TEST 2

DIRECTIONS: Each question or incomplete statement is followed by several suggested answers or completions. Select the one that BEST answers the question or completes the statement. *PRINT THE LETTER OF THE CORRECT ANSWER IN THE SPACE AT THE RIGHT.*

Questions 1-5.

DIRECTIONS: Questions 1 through 5 consist of short paragraphs. Each paragraph contains one word which is INCORRECTLY used because it is NOT in keeping with the meaning of the paragraph. Find the word in each paragraph which is INCORRECTLY used, and then select as the answer the suggested word which should be substituted for the incorrectly used word.

SAMPLE QUESTION

In determining who is to do the work in your unit, you will have to decide just who does what from day to day. One of your lowest responsibilities is to assign work so that everybody gets a fair share and that everyone can do his part well.

A. new B. old C. important D. performance

EXPLANATION

The word which is NOT in keeping with the meaning of the paragraph is "lowest". This is the INCORRECTLY used word. The suggested word "important" would be in keeping with the meaning of the paragraph and should be substituted for "lowest". Therefore, the CORRECT answer is Choice C.

1. If really good practice in the elimination of preventable injuries is to be achieved and held in any establishment, top management must refuse full and definite responsibility and must apply a good share of its attention to the task. 1.____

A. accept B. avoidable C. duties D. problem

2. Recording the human face for identification is by no means the only service performed by the camera in the field of investigation. When the trial of any issue takes place, a word picture is sought to be distorted to the court of incidents, occurrences, or events which are in dispute. 2.____

A. appeals
B. description
C. portrayed
D. deranged

3. In the collection of physical evidence, it cannot be emphasized too strongly that a haphazard systematic search at the scene of the crime is vital. Nothing must be overlooked. Often the only leads in a case will come from the results of this search. 3.____

A. important
B. investigation
C. proof
D. thorough

4. If an investigator has reason to suspect that the witness is mentally stable or a habitual drunkard, he should leave no stone unturned in his investigation to determine if the witness was under the influence of liquor or drugs, or was mentally unbalanced either at the time of the occurrence to which he testified or at the time of the trial. 4.____

A. accused B. clue C. deranged D. question

5. The use of records is a valuable step in crime investigation and is the main reason every department should maintain accurate reports. Crimes are not committed through the use of departmental records alone but from the use of all records, of almost every type, wherever they may be found and whenever they give any incidental information regarding the criminal. 5.___

A. accidental B. necessary C. reported D. solved

Questions 6-8.

DIRECTIONS: Questions 6 through 8 are to be answered SOLELY on the basis of the following passage.

The mass media are an integral part of the daily life of virtually every American. Among these media, the youngest, television, is the most persuasive. Ninety-five percent of American homes have at least one television set, and on the average that set is in use for about 40 hours each week. The central place of television in American life makes this medium the focal point of a growing national concern over the effects of media portrayals of violence on the values, attitudes, and behavior of an ever increasing audience.

In our concern about violence and its causes, it is easy to make television a scapegoat. But we emphasise the fact that there is no simple answer to the problem of violence -- no single explanation of its causes, and no single prescription for its control. It should be remembered that America also experienced high levels of crime and violence in periods before the advent of television.

The problem of balance, taste, and artistic merit in entertaining programs on television are complex. We cannot countenance government censorship of television. Nor would we seek to impose arbitrary limitations on programming which might jeopardize television's ability to deal in dramatic presentations with controversial social issues. Nonetheless, we are deeply troubled by television's constant portrayal of violence, not in any genuine attempt to focus artistic expression on the human condition, but rather in pandering to a public preoccupation with violence that television itself has helped to generate.

6. According to the passage, television uses violence MAINLY 6.___

A. to highlight the reality of everyday existence
B. to satisfy the audience's hunger for destructive action
C. to shape the values and attitudes of the public
D. when it films documentaries concerning human conflict

7. Which one of the following statements is BEST supported by this passage? 7.___

A. Early American history reveals a crime pattern which is not related to television.
B. Programs should give presentations of social issues and never portray violent acts.
C. Television has proven that entertainment programs can easily make the balance between taste and artistic merit a simple matter.
D. Values and behavior should be regulated by governmental censorship.

8. Of the following, which word has the same meaning as countenance as it is used in the above passage? 8.___

A. approve B. exhibit C. oppose D. reject

Questions 9-12.

DIRECTIONS: Questions 9 through 12 are to be answered SOLELY on the basis of the following graph relating to the burglary rate in the city, 2003 to 2008, inclusive.

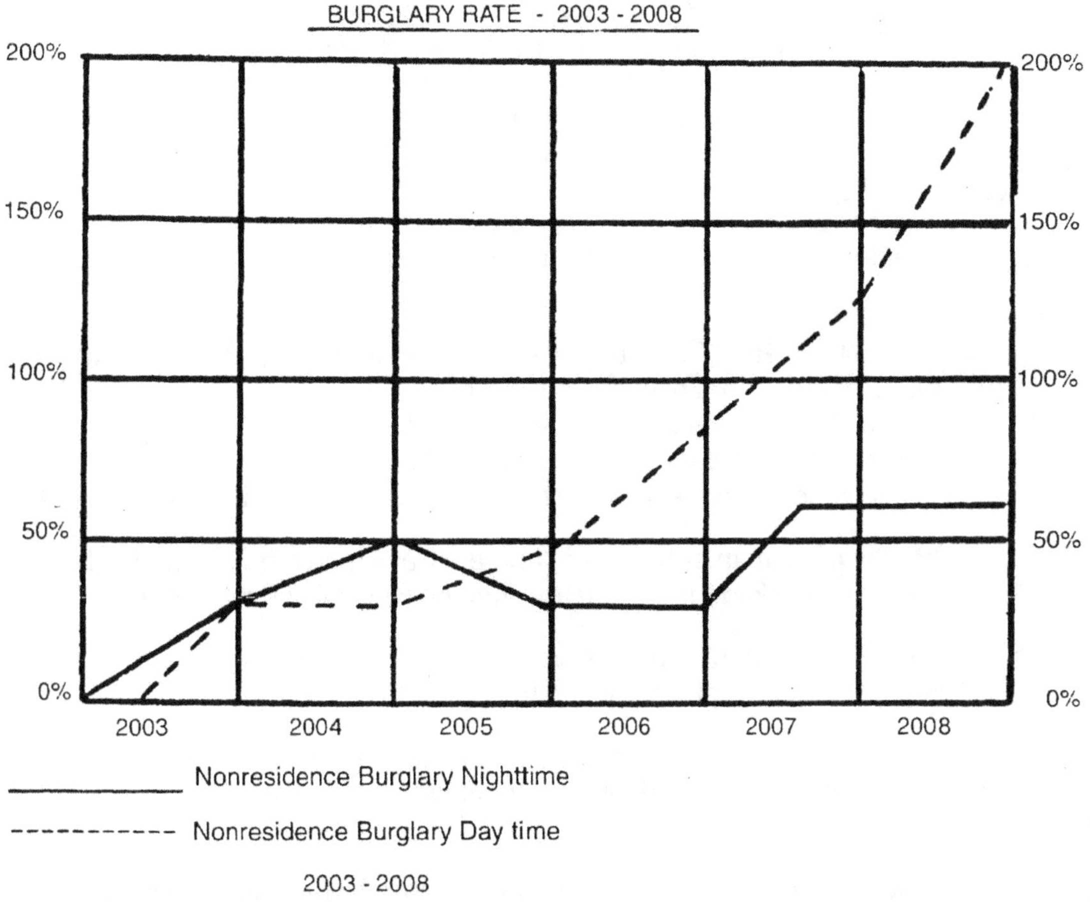

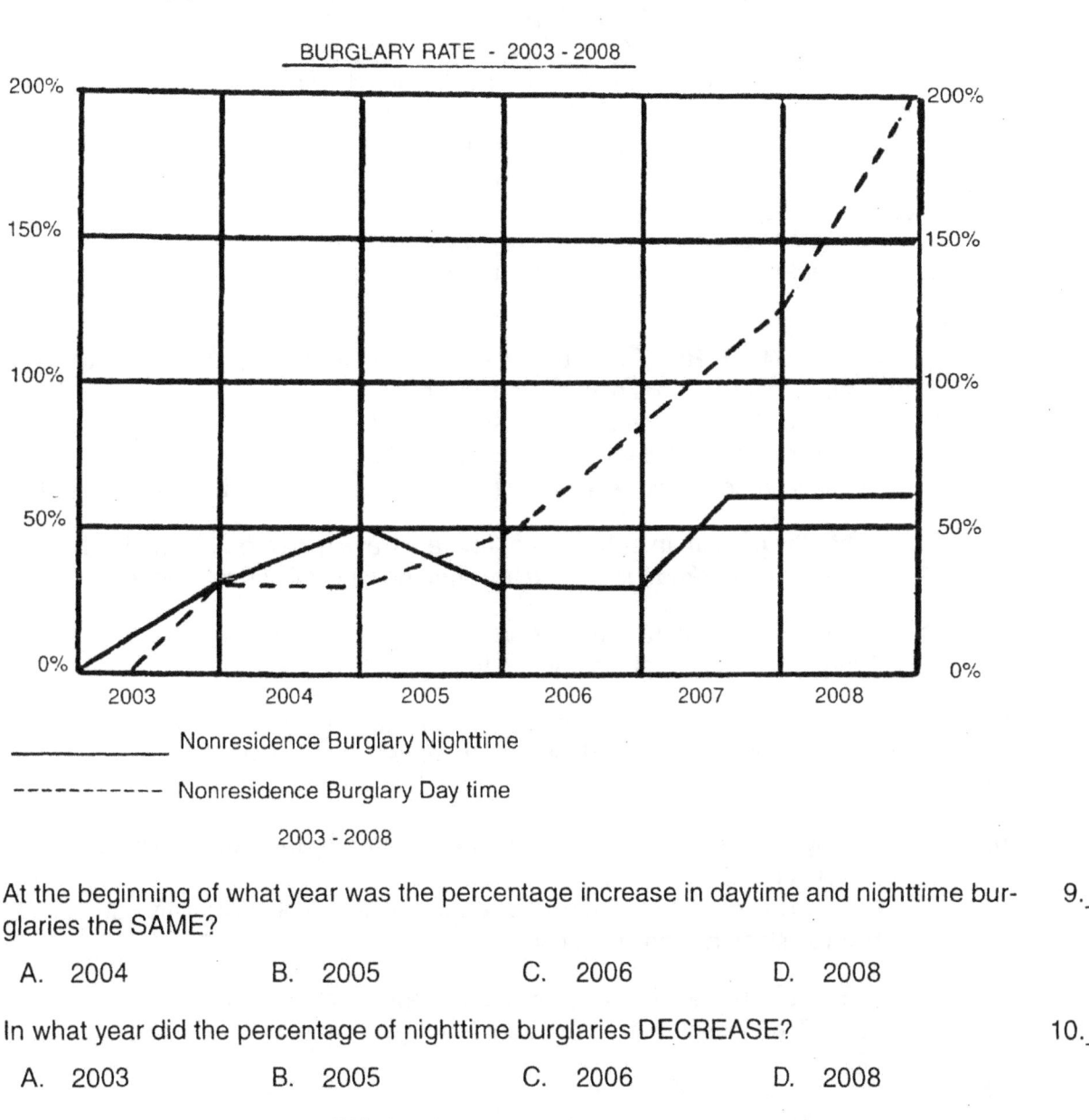

9. At the beginning of what year was the percentage increase in daytime and nighttime burglaries the SAME? 9.____

A. 2004 B. 2005 C. 2006 D. 2008

10. In what year did the percentage of nighttime burglaries DECREASE? 10.____

A. 2003 B. 2005 C. 2006 D. 2008

11. In what year was there the MOST rapid increase in the percentage of daytime non-residence burglaries? 11.____

A. 2004 B. 2006 C. 2007 D. 2008

12. At the end of 2007, the actual number of nighttime burglaries committed 12.____

A. was about 20%
B. was 40%
C. was 400
D. cannot be determined from the information given

Questions 13-17.

DIRECTIONS: Questions 13 through 17 consist of two sentences numbered 1 and 2 taken from police officers' reports. Some of these sentences are correct according to ordinary formal English usage. Other sentences are incorrect because they contain errors in English usage or punctuation. Consider a sentence correct if it contains no errors in English usage or punctuation even if there may be other ways of writing the sentence correctly. Mark your answer to each question in the space at the right as follows:

A. If only sentence 1 is correct, but not sentence 2
B. If only sentence 2 is correct, but not sentence 1
C. If sentences 1 and 2 are both correct
D. If sentences 1 and 2 are both incorrect

SAMPLE QUESTION

1. The woman claimed that the purse was her's.
2. Everyone of the new officers was assigned to a patrol post.

EXPLANATION

Sentence 1 is INCORRECT because of an error in punctuation. The possessive words, "ours, yours, hers, theirs," do not have the apostrophe (').

Sentence 2 is CORRECT because the subject of the sentence is "Everyone" which is singular and requires the singular verb "was assigned".

Since only sentence 2 is correct, but not sentence 1, the CORRECT answer is B.

13. 1. Either the patrolman or his sergeant are always ready to help the public. 13.___
2. The sergeant asked the patrolman when he would finish the report.

14. 1. The injured man could not hardly talk. 14.___
2. Every officer had ought to hand in their reports on time.

15. 1. Approaching the victim of the assault, two large bruises were noticed by me. 15.___
2. The prisoner was arrested for assault, resisting arrest, and use of a deadly weapon.

16. 1. A copy of the orders, which had been prepared by the captain, was given to each patrolman. 16.___
2. It's always necessary to inform an arrested person of his constitutional rights before asking him any questions.

17. 1. To prevent further bleeding, I applied a tourniquet tothe wound. 17.___
2. John Rano a senior officer was on duty at the time of the accident.

Questions 18-25.

DIRECTIONS: Answer each of Questions 18 through 25 SOLELY on the basis of the statement preceding the questions.

18. The criminal is one whose habits have been erroneously developed or, we should say, developed in anti-social patterns, and therefore the task of dealing with him is not one of punishment, but of treatment. 18.___
The basic principle expressed in this statement is BEST illustrated by the

A. emphasis upon rehabilitation in penal institutions
B. prevalence of capital punishment for murder
C. practice of imposing heavy fines for minor violations
D. legal provision for trial by jury in criminal cases

19. The writ of habeas corpus is one of the great guarantees of personal liberty. Of the following, the BEST justification for this statement is that the writ of habeas corpus is frequently used to 19.____

A. compel the appearance in court of witnesses who are outside the state
B. obtain the production of books and records at a criminal trial
C. secure the release of a person improperly held in custody
D. prevent the use of deception in obtaining testimony of reluctant witnesses

20. Fifteen persons suffered effects of carbon dioxide asphyxiation shortly before noon recently in a seventh-floor pressing shop. The accident occurred in a closed room where six steam presses were in operation. Four men and one woman were overcome. 20.____
Of the following, the MOST probable reason for the fact that so many people were affected simultaneously is that

A. women evidently show more resistance to the effects of carbon dioxide than men
B. carbon dioxide is an odorless and colorless gas
C. carbon dioxide is lighter than air
D. carbon dioxide works more quickly at higher altitudes

21. Lay the patient on his stomach, one arm extended directly overhead, the other arm bent at the elbow, and with the face turned outward and resting on hand or forearm. 21.____
To the officer who is skilled at administering first aid, these instructions should IMMEDIATELY suggest

A. application of artificial respiration
B. treatment for third degree burns of the arm
C. setting a dislocated shoulder
D. control of capillary bleeding in the stomach

22. The soda and acid fire extinguisher is the hand extinguisher most commonly used by officers. The main body of the cylinder is filled with a mixture of water and bicarbonate of soda. In a separate interior compartment, at the top, is a small bottle of sulphuric acid. When the extinguisher is inverted, the acid spills into the solution below and starts a chemical reaction. The carbon dioxide thereby generated forces the solution from the extinguisher. 22.____
The officer who understands the operation of this fire extinguisher should know that it is LEAST likely to operate properly

A. in basements or cellars
B. in extremely cold weather
C. when the reaction is of a chemical nature
D. when the bicarbonate of soda is in solution

23. Suppose that, at a training lecture, you are told that many of the men in our penal institutions today are second and third offenders. 23.____
Of the following, the MOST valid inference you can make SOLELY on the basis of this statement is that

A. second offenders are not easily apprehended
B. patterns of human behavior are not easily changed
C. modern laws are not sufficiently flexible
D. laws do not breed crimes

24. In all societies of our level of culture, acts are committed which arouse censure severe enough to take the form of punishment by the government. Such acts are crimes, not because of their inherent nature, but because of their ability to arouse resentment and to stimulate repressive measures. 24.___
Of the following, the MOST valid inference which can be drawn from this statement is that

A. society unjustly punishes acts which are inherently criminal
B. many acts are not crimes but are punished by society because such acts threaten the lives of innocent people
C. only modern society has a level of culture
D. societies sometimes disagree as to what acts are crimes

25. Crime cannot be measured directly. Its amount must be inferred from the frequency of some occurrence connected with it; for example, crimes brought to the attention of the police, persons arrested, prosecutions, convictions, and other dispositions, such as probation or commitment. Each of these may be used as an index of the amount of crime. 25.___
SOLELY on the basis of the foregoing statement, it is MOST correct to state that

A. the incidence of crime cannot be estimated with any accuracy
B. the number of commitments is usually greater than the number of probationary sentences
C. the amount of crime is ordinarily directly correlated with the number of persons arrested
D. a joint consideration of crimes brought to the attention of the police and the number of prosecutions undertaken gives little indication of the amount of crime in a locality

KEY (CORRECT ANSWERS)

1. B
2. A
3. D
4. C
5. D
6. B
7. A
8. A
9. A
10. B
11. D
12. D
13. D
14. D
15. B
16. C
17. A
18. A
19. C
20. B
21. A
22. B
23. B
24. D
25. C

VISUAL RECALL

EXAMINATION SECTION
TEST 1

DIRECTIONS: Each question or incomplete statement is followed by several suggested answers or completions. Select the one that BEST answers the question or completes the statement. *PRINT THE LETTER OF THE CORRECT ANSWER IN THE SPACE AT THE RIGHT.* This test consists of four(4) pictures with questions following each picture. Study each picture for three (3) minutes. Then answer the questions based upon what you remember without looking back at the pictures.

Questions 1-5

DIRECTIONS: Questions 1 through 5 are based on the drawing below showing a view of a waiting area in a public building.

1. A desk is shown in the drawing. Which of the following is on the desk? A(n) 1.____

   A. plant B. telephone
   C. in-out file D. *Information* sign

2. On which floor is the waiting area? 2.____

   A. Basement B. Main floor
   C. Second floor D. Third floor

3. The door immediately to the right of the desk is a(n) 3.____

   A. door to the Personnel Office
   B. elevator door
   C. door to another corridor
   D. door to the stairs

4. Among the magazines on the tables in the waiting area are 4.____

   A. TIME and NEWSWEEK
   B. READER'S DIGEST and T.V. GUIDE
   C. NEW YORK and READER'S DIGEST
   D. TIME and T.V. GUIDE

5. One door is partly open. This is the door to 5.____

   A. the Director's office
   B. the Personnel Manager's office
   C. the stairs
   D. an unmarked office

Questions 6-9.

DIRECTIONS: Questions 6 through 9 are based on the drawing below showing the contents of a male suspect's pockets.

6. The suspect had a slip in his pockets showing an appointment at an out-patient clinic on 6.____

   A. February 9, 2009 B. September 2, 2008
   C. February 19, 2008 D. September 12, 2009

7. The transistor radio that was found on the suspect was made by 7.____

   A. RCA B. GE C. Sony D. Zenith

8. The coins found in the suspect's pockets have a TOTAL value of 8.____

   A. 56¢ B. 77¢ C. $1.05 D. $1.26

9. All except one of the following were found in the suspect's pockets. Which was NOT found? 9.____
   A

   A. ticket stub B. comb
   C. subway token D. pen

Questions 10-13.

DIRECTIONS: Questions 10 through 13 are based on the picture showing the contents of a woman's handbag. Assume that all of the contents are shown in the picture.

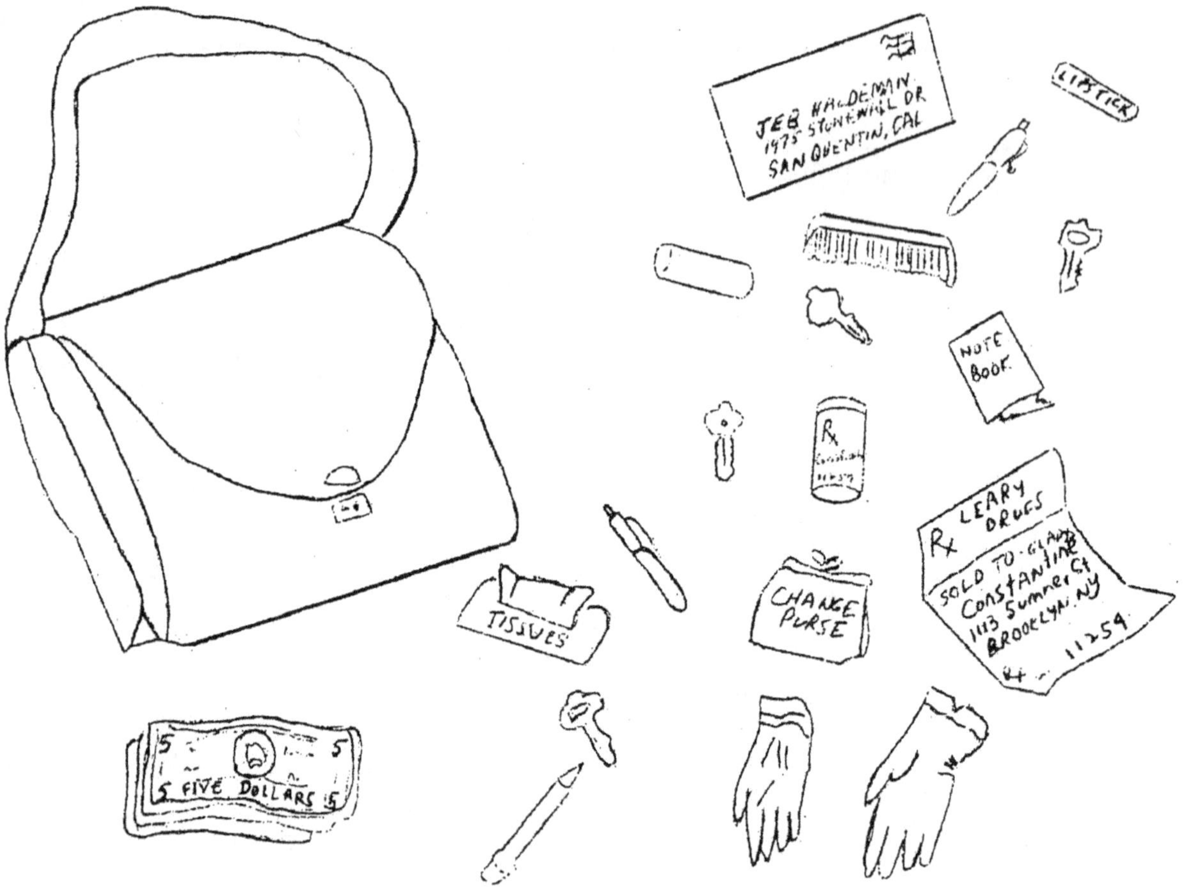

10. Where does Gladys Constantine live? 10.____
_______ Street in _______.

A. Chalmers; Manhattan
B. Summer; Manhattan
C. Summer; Brooklyn
D. Chalmers; Brooklyn

11. How many keys were in the handbag? 11.____

A. 2
B. 3
C. 4
D. 5

12. How much money was in the handbag? 12.____
_______ dollar(s).

A. Exactly five
B. More than five
C. Exactly ten
D. Less than one

13. The sales slip found in the handbag shows the purchase of which of the following? 13.____

A. The handbag
B. Lipstick
C. Tissues
D. Prescription medicine

Questions 14-18.

DIRECTIONS: Questions 14 through 18 are based on the street scene on the following page. A robbery may be in progress down the block from where you are standing. Study and memorize the details before answering these questions.

14. The man carrying the two shopping bags is wearing 14.____

    A. khaki shorts and work boots
    B. a hat and black jacket
    C. a zip-up fleece and glasses
    D. a casual shirt and jeans

15. The building at the center of the photo is a(n) 15.____

    A. hotel B. bank C. restaurant D. office building

16. The sidewalk is lined on the street side with 16.____

    A. parking meters B. safety pillars
    C. street vendors D. flower beds

17. Among the people standing in front of the center building is a 17.____

    A. man wearing khaki pants
    B. woman wearing knee-high boots
    C. young boy chasing another young boy
    D. man wearing a sports jersey

18. Reflections in the store windows indicate that 18.____

A. there are food carts parked in the street
B. a white truck is driving nearby
C. it is a very sunny day
D. a man is sitting on a curb nearby

KEY (CORRECT ANSWERS)

1. D
2. C
3. B
4. D
5. B

6. A
7. C
8. D
9. D
10. C

11. C
12. B
13. D
14. C
15. A

16. D
17. A
18. B

EXAMINATION SECTION
TEST 1

DIRECTIONS: Each question or incomplete statement is followed by several suggested answers or completions. Select the one that BEST answers the question or completes the statement. *PRINT THE LETTER OF THE CORRECT ANSWER IN THE SPACE AT THE RIGHT.*

Questions 1-10. MEMORY

DIRECTIONS: Questions 1 through 10 are to be answered SOLELY on the basis of the following passage, which contains a story about an incident involving police officers. You will have ten minutes to read and study the story. You may not write or make any notes while studying it. After ten minutes, close the memory booklet and do not look at it again. Then, answer the questions that follow.

You are one of a number of police officers who have been assigned to help control a demonstration inside Baldwin Square, a major square in the city. The demonstration is to protest the U.S. involvement in Iraq. As was expected, the demonstration has become nasty. You and nine other officers have been assigned to keep the demonstrators from going up Bell Street which enters the Square from the northwest. During the time you have been assigned to Bell Street, you have observed a number of things.

Before the demonstration began, three vans and a wagon entered the Square from the North on Howard Avenue. The first van was a 1989 blue Ford, plate number 897-JLK. The second van was a 1995 red Ford, plate number 899-LKK. The third van was a 1997 green Dodge step-van, plate number 997-KJL. The wagon was a blue 1998 Volvo with a luggage rack on the roof, plate number 989-LKK. The Dodge had a large dent in the left-hand rear door and was missing its radiator grill. The Ford that was painted red had markings under the paint which made you believe that it had once been a telephone company truck. Equipment for the speakers' platform was unloaded from the van, along with a number of demonstration signs. As soon as the vans and wagon were unloaded, a number of demonstrators picked up the signs and started marching around the square. A sign reading *U.S. Out Now* was carried by a woman wearing red jeans, a black tee shirt, and blue sneakers. A man with a beard, a blue shirt, and Army pants began carrying a poster reading *To Hell With Davis.* A tall, Black male and a Hispanic male had been carrying a large sign with *This Is How Vietnam Started* in big black letters with red dripping off the bottom of each letter.

A number of the demonstrators are wearing black armbands and green tee shirts with the peace symbol on the front. A woman with very short hair who was dressed in green and yellow fatigues is carrying a triangular-shaped blue sign with white letters. The sign says *Out Of Iraq.*

A group of 12 demonstrators have been carrying six fake coffins back and forth across the Square between Apple Street on the West and Webb Street on the East. They are shouting *Death to Hollis and his Henchmen.* Over where Victor Avenue enters the Square from the South, a small group of demonstrators (two men and three women) just started painting slogans on the walls surrounding the construction of the First National Union Bank and Trust.

1. Which street is on the opposite side of the Square from Victor Avenue? 1.____
   A. Bell B. Howard C. Apple D. Webb

2. How many officers are assigned with you? 2.____
   A. 8 B. 6 C. 9 D. 5

3. Howard Avenue enters the Square from which direction? 3.____
   A. Northwest B. North C. East D. Southwest

4. The van that had PROBABLY been a telephone truck had plate number 4.____
   A. 899-LKK B. 989-LKK C. 897-JKL D. 997-KJL

5. What is the color of the sign carried by the woman with very short hair? 5.____
   A. Blue B. White C. Black D. Red

6. The man wearing the army pants has a(n) 6.____
   A. Afro
   B. beard
   C. triangular-shaped sign
   D. black armband

7. Which vehicle had plate number 989-LKK? The 7.____
   A. red Ford B. blue Ford C. Volvo D. Dodge

8. The bank under construction is located ______ of the Square. 8.____
   A. north B. south C. east D. west

9. How many people are painting slogans on the walls surrounding the construction site? 9.____
   A. 4 B. 5 C. 6 D. 7

10. What is the name of the bank under construction? 10.____
    A. National Union Bank and Trust
    B. First National Bank and Trust
    C. First Union National Bank and Trust
    D. First National Union Bank and Trust

KEY (CORRECT ANSWERS)

1. B
2. C
3. B
4. A
5. A
6. B
7. C
8. B
9. B
10. D

TEST 2

DIRECTIONS: Each question or incomplete statement is followed by several suggested answers or completions. Select the one that BEST answers the question or completes the statement. *PRINT THE LETTER OF THE CORRECT ANSWER IN THE SPACE AT THE RIGHT.*

Questions 1-15.

DIRECTIONS: Questions 1 through 15 are to be answered SOLELY on the basis of the Memory Booklet given below.

MEMORY BOOKLET

The following passage contains a story about an incident involving police officers. You will have ten minutes to read and study the story. You may not write or make any notes while studying it. The first questions in the examination will be based on the passage. After ten minutes, close the memory booklet, and do not look at it again. Then, answer the questions that follow.

Police Officers Boggs and Thomas are patrolling in a radio squad car on a late Saturday afternoon in the spring. They are told by radio that a burglary is taking place on the top floor of a six-story building on the corner of 5th Street and Essex and that they should deal with the incident.

The police officers know the location and know that the Gold Jewelry Company occupies the entire sixth floor. They also know that, over the weekends, the owner has gold bricks in his office safe worth $500,000.

When the officers arrive at the location, they lock their radio car. They then find the superintendent of the building who opens the front door for them. He indicates he has neither seen nor heard anything suspicious in the building. However, he had just returned from a long lunch hour. The officers take the elevator to the sixth floor. As the door of the elevator with the officers opens on the sixth floor, the officers hear the door of the freight elevator in the rear of the building closing and the freight elevator beginning to move. They leave the elevator and proceed quickly through the open door of the office of the Gold Jewelry Company. They see that the office safe is open and empty. The officers quickly proceed to the rear staircase. They run down six flights of stairs, and they see four suspects leaving through the rear entrance of the building.

They run through the rear door and out of the building after the suspects. The four suspects are running quickly through the parking lot at the back of the building. The suspects then make a right-hand turn onto 5th Street and are clearly seen by the officers. The officers see one white male, one Hispanic male, one Black male, and one white female.

The white male has a beard and sunglasses. He is wearing blue jeans, a dark red and blue jacket, and white jogging shoes. He is carrying a large green duffel bag over his shoulder.

The Hispanic male limps slightly and has a dark moustache. He is wearing dark brown slacks, a dark green sweat shirt, and brown shoes. He is carrying a large blue duffel bag.

The Black male is clean-shaven, wearing black corduroy pants, a multi-colored shirt, a green beret, and black boots. He is carrying a tool box.

The white female has long dark hair and is wear-ing light-colored blue jeans, a white blouse, sneakers, and a red kerchief around her neck. She is carrying a shotgun.

The officers chase the suspects for three long blocks without getting any closer to them. At the intersection of 5th Street and Pennsylvania Avenue, the suspects separate. The white male and the Black male rapidly get into a 1992 brown Ford stationwagon. The stationwagon has a roof rack on top and a Connecticut license plate with the letters *JEAN* on it. The stationwagon departs even before the occupants close the door completely.

The Hispanic male and the white female get into an old blue Dodge van. The van has a CB antenna on top, a picture of a cougar on the back doors, a dented right rear fender, and a New Jersey license plate. The officers are not able to read the plate numbers on the van.

The officers then observe the stationwagon turn left and enter an expressway going to Connecticut. The van turns right onto Illinois Avenue and proceeds toward the tunnel to New Jersey.

The officers immediately run back to their radio car to radio in what happened.

1. Which one of the following suspects had sunglasses on? 1.____

   A. White male B. Hispanic male
   C. Black male D. White female

2. Which one of the following suspects was carrying a shotgun? 2.____

   A. White male B. Hispanic male
   C. Black male D. White female

3. Which one of the following suspects was wearing a green beret? 3.____

   A. White male B. Hispanic male
   C. Black male D. White femal

4. Which one of the following suspects limped slightly? 4.____

   A. White male B. Hispanic male
   C. Black male D. White female

5. Which one of the following BEST describes the stationwagon used? 5.____
   A

   A. 1992 brown Ford B. 1992 blue Dodge
   C. 1979 brown Ford D. 1979 blue Dodge

6. Which one of the following BEST describes the suspect or suspects who used the stationwagon? A 6.____

A. Black male and a Hispanic male
B. white male and a Hispanic male
C. Black male and a white male
D. Black male and a white female

7. The van had a license plate from which of the following states? 7.____

A. Connecticut
B. New Jersey
C. New York
D. Pennsylvania

8. The license plate on the stationwagon read as follows: 8.____

A. JANE
B. JOAN
C. JEAN
D. JUNE

9. The van used had a dented ______ fender. 9.____

A. left rear
B. right rear
C. right front
D. left front

10. When last seen by the officers, the van was headed toward 10.____

A. Connecticut
B. New Jersey
C. Pennsylvania
D. Long Island

11. The female suspect's hair can BEST be described as 11.____

A. long and dark-colored
B. short and dark-colored
C. long and light-colored
D. short and light-colored

12. Which one of the following suspects was wearing a multicolored shirt? 12.____

A. White male
B. Hispanic male
C. Black male
D. White female

13. Blue jeans were worn by the ______ male suspect and the suspect. 13.____

A. Hispanic; white female
B. Black; Hispanic male
C. white; white female
D. Black; white male

14. The color of the duffel bag carried by the Hispanic male suspect was 14.____

A. blue
B. green
C. brown
D. red

15. The Hispanic male suspect was wearing 15.____

A. brown shoes
B. black shoes
C. black boots
D. jogging shoes

KEY (CORRECT ANSWERS)

1. A
2. D
3. C
4. B
5. A
6. C
7. B
8. C
9. B
10. B
11. A
12. C
13. C
14. A
15. A

READING COMPREHENSION
UNDERSTANDING AND INTERPRETING WRITTEN MATERIAL

EXAMINATION SECTION
TEST 1

DIRECTIONS: Each question or incomplete statement is followed by several suggested answers or completions. Select the one that BEST answers the question or completes the statement. *PRINT THE LETTER OF THE CORRECT ANSWER IN THE SPACE AT THE RIGHT.*

1. Custody in prison work used to be considered of such supreme importance that everything else was secondary. This statement implies MOST directly that 1.____

   A. formerly nothing was as important as custody in prison work
   B. formerly only custody was considered important in prison work
   C. today all aspects of prison work are considered equally important
   D. today reform of the prisoner is considered more important than custody

2. Since the total inmate treatment and training program is conditioned largely by custody requirements, its success is almost wholly dependent on flexibility of custody classification and handling of prisoners. 2.____
   Of the following, the MOST accurate statement based on the above statement is that the

   A. conditions of custody are completely dependent on the handling of inmates in accordance with their classification
   B. daily schedule at the institution should be flexible in order for the treatment and training program to succeed
   C. main factor influencing the inmate treatment and training program is the requirement for the proper safekeeping of inmates
   D. most important factor in the success of the treatment and training program is the cooperation of the inmates

3. An officer's revolver is a defensive and not offensive weapon. 3.____
   On the basis of this statement only, an officer should BEST draw his revolver to

   A. fire at an unarmed burglar
   B. force a suspect to confess
   C. frighten a juvenile delinquent
   D. protect his own life

4. Prevention of crime is of greater value to the community than the punishment of crime. 4.____
   If this statement is accepted as true, GREATEST emphasis should be placed on

   A. malingering
   B. medication
   C. imprisonment
   D. rehabilitation

5. The criminal is rarely or never reformed. Acceptance of this statement as true would mean that GREATEST emphasis should be placed on 5.____

   A. imprisonment
   B. parole
   C. probation
   D. malingering

6. Physical punishment of prison inmates has been shown by experience not only to be ineffective but to be dangerous and, in the long run, destructive of good discipline. According to the preceding statement, it is MOST reasonable to assume that, in the supervision of prison inmates, 6.____

   A. a good correction officer would not use physical punishment
   B. it is permissible for a good correction officer to use a limited amount of physical punishment to enforce discipline
   C. physical punishment improves discipline temporarily
   D. the danger of public scandal is basic in cases where physical punishment is used

7. There is no clear evidence that criminals, as a group, differ from non-criminals in their basic psychological needs.
   On the basis of this statement, it is MOST reasonable to assume that criminals and non-criminals 7.____

   A. are alike in some important respects
   B. are alike in their respective backgrounds
   C. differ but slightly in all respects
   D. differ in physical characteristics

8. Neither immediate protection for the community nor long-range reformation of the prisoner can be achieved by prison personnel who express toward the offender whatever feelings of frustration, fear, jealousy, or hunger for power they may have.
   Of the following, the CHIEF significance of this statement for correction officers is that, in their daily work, they should 8.____

   A. be on the constant lookout for opportunities to prove their courage to inmates
   B. not allow deeply personal problems to affect their relations with the inmates
   C. not try to advance themselves on the job because of personal motives
   D. spend a good part of their time examining their own feelings in order to understand better those of the inmates

9. Since ninety-five percent of prison inmates are released, and a great majority of these within two to three years, a prison which does nothing more than separate the criminal from society offers little promise of real protection to society.
   Of the following, the MOST valid reference which may be drawn from the preceding statement is that 9.____

   A. once it has been definitely established that a person has criminal tendencies, that person should be separated for the rest of his life from ordinary society
   B. prison sentences in general are much too short and should be lengthened to afford greater protection to society
   C. punishment, rather than separation of the criminal from society, should be the major objective of a correctional prison
   D. when a prison system produces no change in prisoners, and the period of imprisonment is short, the period during which society is protected is also short

10. A great handicap to successful correctional work lies in the negative response of the general community to the offender. Public attitudes of hostility toward, and rejection of, an ex-prisoner can undo the beneficial effects of even an ideal correctional system. Of the following, the CHIEF implication of this statement is that 10.____

   A. a friendly community attitude will insure the successful reformation of the ex-prisoner
   B. correctional efforts with most prisoners would generally prove successful if it were not for public hostility toward the former inmate
   C. in the long run, even an ideal correctional system cannot successfully reform criminals
   D. the attitude of the community toward an ex-prisoner is an important factor in determining whether or not an ex-prisoner reforms

11. While retribution and deterrence as a general philosophy in correction are widely condemned, no one raises any doubt as to the necessity for secure custody of some criminals. Of the following, the MOST valid conclusion based on the preceding statement is that the 11.____

   A. gradual change in the philosophy of correction has not affected custody practices
   B. need for safe custody of some criminals is not questioned by anyone
   C. philosophy of retribution, as shown in some correctional systems, has led to wide condemnation of custodial practices applied to all types of criminals

Questions 12-13.

DIRECTIONS: Questions 12 and 13 are to be answered SOLELY on the basis of the information contained in the following paragraph.

Those correction theorists who are in agreement with severe and rigid controls as a normal part of the correctional process are confronted with a contradiction; this is so because a responsibility which is consistent with freedom cannot be developed in a repressive atmosphere. They do not recognize this contradiction when they carry out their programs with dictatorial force and expect convicted criminals exposed to such programs to be reformed into free and responsible citizens.

12. According to the above paragraph, those correction theorists are faced with a contradiction who 12.____

   A. are in favor of the enforcement of strict controls in a prison
   B. believe that to develop a sense of responsibility, freedom must not be restricted
   C. take the position that the development of responsibility consistent with freedom is not possible in a repressive atmosphere
   D. think that freedom and responsibility can be developed only in a democratic atmosphere

13. According to the above paragraph, a repressive atmosphere in a prison 13.____

   A. does not conform to present day ideas of freedom of the individual
   B. is admitted by correction theorists to be in conflict with the basic principles of the normal correctional process

C. is advocated as the best method of maintaining discipline when rehabilitation is of secondary importance
D. is not suitable for the development of a sense of responsibility consistent with freedom

14. To state the matter in simplest terms, just as surely as some people are inclined to commit crimes, so some people are prevented from committing crimes by the fear of the consequences to themselves. 14.___
Of the following, the MOST logical conclusion based on this statement is that

A. as many people are prevented from committing criminal acts as actually commit criminal acts
B. most men are not inclined to commit crimes
C. people who are inclined to violate the law are usually deterred from their purpose
D. there are people who have a tendency to commit crimes and people who are deterred from crime

15. Probation is a judicial instrument whereby a judge may withhold execution of a sentence upon a convicted person in order to give opportunity for rehabilitation in the community under the guidance of an officer of the court. According to the preceding statement, it is MOST reasonable to assume that 15.___

A. a person on probation must report to the court at least once a month
B. a person who has been convicted of crime is sometimes placed on probation by the judge
C. criminals who have been rehabilitated in the community are placed on probation by the court after they are sentenced
D. the chief purpose of probation is to make the sentence easier to serve

Questions 16-19.

DIRECTIONS: Questions 16 through 19 are to be answered SOLELY on the basis of the following passage.

Traditional correctional institutions do not change or redirect the behavior of many of their inmates. Few of these establishments are equipped with adequate resources to treat the social and psychological handicaps of their wards. Too often, far removed ideologically from the world to which its charges must return, the institution often compounds the problems its corrective mechanisms are intended to cure. Training school academic programs, for example, range from poor to totally inadequate and usually reinforce negative feelings toward future learning experiences. Vocational programs are frequently designed to benefit the institution without regard to the inmate, and the usual low-key common denominator *treatment* program scarcely begins to meet the needs of many offenders.

Most correctional institutions must mobilize their limited resources in time and talent for purposes other than the ever-present concern about runaways or escapes. No one could quarrel rationally with the need to safeguard the community and control the behavior of people who may be of danger to themselves or others. It is ridiculous and tragic, however, that an overstated security approach is still the rule for the bulk of our correctional population.

16. The passage states that inmates of traditional correctional institutions are LIKELY to 16.____
    A. develop belief in radical political ideologies
    B. experience conditions that produce no betterment
    C. give major attention to devising plans of escape
    D. desire vocational training unrelated to their individual potential

17. The passage indicates that traditional training school academic programs lead inmates to 17.____
    A. adjust to the institutional setting
    B. avoid later formal learning
    C. develop respect for the values of education
    D. request more practical, vocational training

18. The passage indicates that most traditional correctional institutions, because of their ideological distance from the realities of the outside world, are MOST likely to 18.____
    A. ignore the safety of the outside community
    B. favor a minority of the inmate population
    C. lack properly motivated staff
    D. increase the problems of inmates

19. The passage states that the strong custodial function in most correctional institutions is MOST likely to be 19.____
    A. accorded excessive emphasis
    B. aimed at incorrigible inmates only
    C. necessary to redirect inmate behavior
    D. resented by the outside community

Questions 20-22.

DIRECTIONS: Questions 20 through 22 are to be answered SOLELY on the basis of the following passage.

The most widely accepted argument in favor of the death penalty is that the threat of its infliction deters people from committing capital offenses. Of course, since human behavior can be influenced through fear, and since man tends to fear death, it is possible to use capital punishment as a deterrent. But the real question is whether individuals think of the death penalty BEFORE they act, and whether they are thereby deterred from committing crimes. If for the moment we assume that the death penalty does this to some extent, we must also grant that certain human traits limit its effectiveness as a deterrent. Man tends to be a creature of habit and emotion, and when he is handicapped by poverty, ignorance, and malnutrition, as criminals often are, he becomes notoriously shortsighted. Many violators of the law give little thought to the possibility of detection and apprehension, and often they do not even consider the penalty. Moreover, it appears that most people do not regulate their lives in terms of the pleasure and pain that may result from their acts.

Human nature is very complex. A criminal may fear punishment, but he may fear the anger and contempt of his companions or his family even more, and the fear of economic insecurity or exclusion from the group whose respect he cherishes may drive him to commit the most daring crimes. Besides, fear is not the only emotion that motivates man. Love, loyalty, ambition, greed, lust, anger, and resentment may steel him to face even death in the perpetration of crime, and impel him to devise the most ingenious methods to get what he wants and to avoid detection.

If the death penalty were surely, quickly, uniformly, publicly, and painfully inflicted, it undoubtedly would prevent many capital offenses that are being committed by those who do consider the punishment that they may receive for their crimes. But this is precisely the point. Certainly, the way in which the death penalty has been administered in the United States is not fitted to produce this result.

20. Of the following, the MOST appropriate title for the above passage is 20.____

    A. CAPITAL OFFENSES IN THE UNITED STATES
    B. THE DEATH PENALTY AS A DETERRENT
    C. HUMAN NATURE AND FEAR
    D. EMOTION AS A CAUSE OF CRIME

21. The above passage implies that the death penalty, as it has been administered in the United States, 21.____

    A. was too prompt and uniform to be effective
    B. deterred many criminals who considered the possible consequences of their actions
    C. prevented crimes primarily among habitual criminals
    D. failed to prevent the commission of many capital offenses

22. According to the above passage, many violators of the law are 22.____

    A. intensely concerned with the pleasure or pain that may result from their acts
    B. influenced primarily by economic factors
    C. not influenced by the opinions of their family or friends
    D. not seriously concerned with the possibility of apprehension

Questions 23-25.

DIRECTIONS: Questions 23 through 25 are to be answered SOLELY on the basis of the information contained in the following paragraph.

As a secondary aspect of this revolutionary change in outlook resulting from the introduction of group counseling into the adult correctional institution, there must evolve a new type of prison employee, the true correctional or treatment worker. The top management will have to reorient their attitudes toward subordinate employees, respecting and accepting them as equal participants in the work of the institution. Rank may no longer be the measure of value in the inmate treatment program. Instead, the employee will be valuable whatever his location in the prison hierarchy or administrative plan in terms of his capacity constructively to relate himself to inmates as one human being to another. In group counseling, all employees must consider it their primary task to provide a wholesome environment for personality growth for the inmates in work crews, cell blocks, clerical pools, or classrooms. The above does not mean that custodial care and precautions regarding the prevention of disorders or escapes are cast aside or discarded by prison workers. On the contrary, the staff will be more acutely aware of the costs to the inmates of such infractions of institutional rules. Gradually, it is hoped, these instances of uncontrolled responses to over-powering feelings by inmates will become much less frequent in the treatment institution, In general, men in group counseling provide considerably fewer disciplinary infractions when compared with a control group of those still on a waiting list to enter group counseling, and especially fewer than those who do not choose to participate. It is optimistically anticipated that some day men in prison may have the same attitudes toward the staff, the same security in expecting treatment as do patients in a good general hospital.

23. According to the above paragraph, under a program of group counseling in an adult correctional institution, that employee will be MOST valuable in the inmate treatment program who 23.____

A. can establish a constructive relationship of one human being to another between himself and the inmate
B. gets top management to accept him as an equal participant in the work of the institution
C. is in contact with the inmate in work crews, cell blocks, clerical pools or classrooms
D. provides the inmate with a proper home environment for wholesome personality growth

24. According to the above paragraph, an effect that the group counseling program is expected to have on the problem of custody and discipline in a prison is that the staff will 24.____

A. be more acutely aware of the cost of maintaining strict prison discipline
B. discard old and outmoded notions of custodial care and the prevention of disorders and escapes
C. neglect this aspect of prison work unless proper safeguards are established
D. realize more deeply the harmful effect on the inmate of breaches of discipline

25. According to the above paragraph, a result that is expected from the group counseling method of inmate treatment in an adult correctional institution is 25.____

A. a greater desire on the part of potential delinquents to enter the correctional institution for the purpose of securing treatment
B. a large reduction in the number of infractions of institutional rules by inmates
C. a steady decrease in the crime rate
D. the introduction of hospital methods of organization and operation into the correctional institution

KEY (CORRECT ANSWERS)

1. A
2. C
3. D
4. D
5. A

6. A
7. A
8. B
9. D
10. D

11. B
12. A
13. D
14. D
15. B

16. B
17. B
18. D
19. A
20. B

21. D
22. D
23. A
24. D
25. B

TEST 2

DIRECTIONS: Each question or incomplete statement is followed by several suggested answers or completions. Select the one that BEST answers the question or completes the statement. *PRINT THE LETTER OF THE CORRECT ANSWER IN THE SPACE AT THE RIGHT.*

Questions 1-7.

DIRECTIONS: Questions 1 through 7 are to be answered on the basis of the following paragraph.

FLAGGING RULES

When a track gang is going to work under flagging protection at a given location, the Desk Trainmaster of the division must be notified. Work on trainways must not be performed on operating tracks between 6:00 A.M. and 9:00 A.M., or between 4:00 P.M. and 7:00 P.M. A flagman must be selected from the list of flagmen qualified as such by the Assistant General Superintendent. No person acting as a flagman may be assigned any duties other than those of a flagman. For underground flagging signals, lighted lanterns must be used. Out of doors, flags at least 23" x 29" in dimensions must be used between sunrise and sunset. Moving a red light across the track is the prescribed stop signal under normal flagging conditions. Moving a white light up and down means proceed slowly. A red light must never be used to give a proceed signal. Moving a yellow light up and down is a signal to a motorman to proceed very slowly. On the track to be worked on, two yellow lights must be displayed at a point not less than 500 feet, nor more than 700 feet, in approach to the flagman's station. On any track where caution lights are displayed, one green light must be displayed a safe distance beyond the farthest point of work. Caution lights must be displayed on the right hand side of the track.

1. Before starting work on a track, the transit official who should be notified is the 1.____

   A. General Superintendent
   B. Assistant General Superintendent
   C. Desk Trainmaster
   D. Yardmaster

2. It is permissible to start work on an operating track at 2.____

   A. 8 A.M. B. 11 A.M. C. 8 P.M. D. 6 P.M.

3. A flagman for a track gang MUST be selected from 3.____

   A. men on light duty
   B. disabled men
   C. a list of qualified men
   D. senior trackmen

4. The flagman who is protecting a working gang of trackmen 4.____

   A. should lend a hand when needed in heavy lifting
   B. should clean up the track area while awaiting trains
   C. must not be assigned to other duties
   D. can collect scrap iron while awaiting trains

5. The prescribed *stop* signal is given by moving a 5.____

   A. red light up and down
   B. green light up and down
   C. red light across the tracks
   D. green light across the tracks

6. The normal *proceed slowly* signal is given by moving a 6.___

   A. red light up and down
   B. white light up and down
   C. yellow light across the tracks
   D. green light across the tracks

7. Of the following, an ACCEPTABLE distance between a work area and the yellow lights is _______ feet. 7.___

   A. 300 B. 600 C. 800 D. 1,000

Questions 8-12.

DIRECTIONS: Questions 8 through 12 are to be answered on the basis of the following passage.

The handling of supplies is an important part of correctional administration. A good deal of planning and organization is involved in purchase, stock control, and issue of bulk supplies to the cell-block. This planning is meaningless, however, if the final link in the chain -- the cell-block officer who is in charge of distributing supplies to the inmates -- does not do his job in the proper way. First, when supplies are received, the officer himself should immediately check them or should personally supervise the checking, to make sure the count is correct. Nothing but trouble will result if an officer signs for 200 towels and discovers hours later that he is 20 towels short. Did the 20 towels *disappear,* or did they never arrive in the first place? Second, all supplies should be locked up until they are actually distributed. Third, the officer must keep accurate records when supplies are issued. Complaints will be kept to a minimum if the officer makes sure that each inmate has received the supplies to which he is entitled, and if the officer can tell from his records when it is time to reorder to prevent a shortage. Fourth, the officer should either issue the supplies himself or else personally supervise the issuing. It is unfair and unwise to put an inmate in charge of supplies without giving him adequate supervision. A small thing like a bar of soap does not mean much to most people, but it means a great deal to the inmate who cannot even shave or wash up unless he receives the soap that is supposed to be issued to him.

8. Which one of the following jobs is NOT mentioned by the above passage as the responsibility of a cellblock officer? 8.___

   A. Purchasing supplies
   B. Issuing supplies
   C. Counting supplies when they are delivered to the cell-block
   D. Keeping accurate records when supplies are issued

9. The above passage says that supplies should be counted when they are delivered. Of the following, which is the BEST way of handling this job? 9.___

   A. The cellblock officer can wait until he has some free time, and then count them himself.
   B. An inmate can start counting them right away, even if the cellblock officer cannot supervise his work.
   C. The cellblock officer can personally supervise an inmate who counts the supplies when they are delivered.
   D. Two inmates can count them when they are delivered, supervising each other's work.

10. The above passage gives an example concerning a delivery of 200 towels that turned out to be 20 towels short. The example is used to show that 10.____

  A. the missing towels were stolen
  B. the missing towels never arrived in the first place
  C. it is impossible to tell what happened to the missing towels because no count was made when they were delivered
  D. it does not matter that the missing towels were not accounted for because it is never possible to keep track of supplies accurately

11. The MAIN reason given by the above passage for making a record when supplies are issued is that keeping records 11.____

  A. will discourage inmates from stealing supplies
  B. is a way of making sure that each inmate receives the supplies to which he is entitled
  C. will show the officer's superiors that he is doing his job in the proper way
  D. will enable the inmates to help themselves to any supplies they need

12. The above passage says that it is unfair to put an inmate in charge of supplies without giving him adequate supervision. 12.____
Which of the following is the MOST likely explanation of why it would be *unfair* to do this?

  A. A privilege should not be given to one inmate unless it is given to all the other inmates too.
  B. It is wrong to make one inmate work when all the others can sit in their cells and do nothing.
  C. The cellblock officer should not be able to get out of doing a job by making an inmate do it for him.
  D. The inmate in charge of supplies could be put under pressure by other inmates to do them *special favors.*

Questions 13-17.

DIRECTIONS: Questions 13 through 17 are to be answered on the basis of the following passage.

The typical correction official must make predictions about the probable future behavior of his charges in order to make judgments affecting those individuals. In learning to predict behavior, the results of scientific studies of inmate behavior can be of some use. Most studies that have been made show that older men tend to obey rules and regulations better than younger men, and tend to be more reliable in carrying out assigned jobs. Men who had good employment records on the outside also tend to be more reliable than men whose records show haphazard employment or unemployment. Oddly enough, men convicted of crimes of violence are less likely to be troublemakers than men convicted of burglary or other crimes involving stealth. While it might be expected that first offenders would be much less likely to be troublemakers than men with previous convictions, the difference between the two groups is not very great. It must be emphasized, however, that predictions based on a man's background are only likelihoods -- they are never certainties. A successful correction officer learns to give some weight to a man's background, but he should rely even more heavily on his own personal judgment of the individual in question. A good officer will develop in time a kind of sixth sense about human beings that is more reliable than any statistical predictions.

13. The above passage suggests that knowledge of scientific studies of inmate behavior would PROBABLY help the correction officer to 13.___

A. make judgments that affect the inmates in his charge
B. write reports on all major infractions of the rules
C. accurately analyze how an inmate's behavior is determined by his background
D. change the personalities of the individuals in his charge

14. According to the information in the above passage, which one of the following groups of inmates would tend to be MOST reliable in carrying out assigned jobs? 14.___

A. Older men with haphazard employment records
B. Older men with regular employment records
C. Younger men with haphazard employment records
D. Younger men with regular employment records

15. According to the information in the above passage, which of the following are MOST likely to be troublemakers? 15.___

A. Older men convicted of crimes of violence
B. Younger men convicted of crimes of violence
C. Younger men convicted of crimes involving stealth
D. First offenders convicted of crimes of violence

16. The above passage indicates that information about a man's background is 16.___

A. a sure way of predicting his future behavior
B. of no use at all in predicting his future behavior
C. more useful in predicting behavior than a correction officer's expert judgment
D. less reliable in predicting behavior than a correction officer's expert judgment

17. The above passage names two groups of inmates whose behavior might be expected to be quite different, but who in fact behave only slightly differently.
These two groups are 17.___

A. older men and younger men
B. first offenders and men with previous convictions
C. men with good employment records and men with records of haphazard employment or unemployment
D. men who obey the rules and men who do not

Questions 18-22.

DIRECTIONS: Questions 18 through 22 are to be answered on the basis of the following passage.

A large proportion of the people who are behind bars are not convicted criminals, but people who have been arrested and are being held until their trial in court. Experts have often pointed out that this detention system does not operate fairly. For instance, a person who can afford to pay bail usually will not get locked up. The theory of the bail system is that the person will make sure to show up in court when he is supposed to since he knows that otherwise he will forfeit his bail -- he will lose the money he put up. Sometimes a person who can show that he is a stable citizen with a job and a family will be released on *personal recognizance* (without bail). The result is that the well-to-do, the employed, and the family men can often avoid the detention system. The people who do wind up in detention tend to be the poor, the unemployed, the single, and the young.

18. According to the above passage, people who are put behind bars 18.____

    A. are almost always dangerous criminals
    B. include many innocent people who have been arrested by mistake
    C. are often people who have been arrested but have not yet come to trial
    D. are all poor people who tend to be young and single

19. The above passage says that the detention system works UNFAIRLY against people 19.____

    A. rich B. married C. old D. unemployed

20. The above passage uses the expression *forfeit his bail*. Even if you have not seen the word *forfeit* before, you could figure out from the way it is used in the passage that *forfeiting* PROBABLY means _________ something. 20.____

    A. losing track of B. giving up
    C. finding D. avoiding

21. When someone is released on *personal recognizance*, this means that 21.____

    A. the judge knows that he is innocent
    B. he does not have to show up for a trial
    C. he has a record of previous convictions
    D. he does not have to pay bail

22. Suppose that two men were booked on the same charge at the same time, and that the same bail was set for both of them. One man was able to put up bail, and he was released. The second man was not able to put up bail, and he was held in detention. The reader of the above passage would MOST likely feel that this result is 22.____

    A. *unfair*, because it does not have any relation to guilt or innocence
    B. *unfair*, because the first man deserves severe punishment
    C. *fair*, because the first man is obviously innocent
    D. *fair*, because the law should be tougher on poor people than on rich people

Questions 23-25.

DIRECTIONS: Questions 23 through 25 are to be answered on the basis of the information contained in the following paragraph,

Group counseling may contain potentialities of an extraordinary character for the philosophy and especially the management and operation of the adult correctional institution. Primarily, the change may be based upon the valued and respected participation of the rank-and-file of employees in the treatment program. Group counseling provides new treatment functions for correctional workers. The older, more conventional duties and activities of correctional officers, teachers, maintenance foremen, and other employees, which they currently perform, may be fortified and improved by their participation in group counseling. Psychologists, psychiatrists, and classification officers may also need to revise their attitudes toward others on the staff and toward their own procedure in treating inmates to accord with the new type of treatment program which may evolve if group counseling were to become accepted practice in the prison. The primary locale of the psychological treatment program may move from the clinical center to all places in the institution where inmates are in contact with employees. The thoughtful guidance and steering of the program, figuratively its pilot-house, may still be the clinical center. The actual points of contact of the treatment program will, however, be wherever inmates are in personal relationship, no matter how superficial, with employees of the prison.

23. According to the above paragraph, a basic change that may be brought about by the introduction of a group counseling program into an adult correctional institution would be that the 23.____

A. educational standards for correctional employees would be raised
B. management of the institution would have to be selected primarily on the basis of ability to understand and apply the counseling program
C. older and conventional duties of correctional employees would assume less importance
D. rank-and-file employees would play an important part in the treatment program for inmates

24. According to the above paragraph, the one of the following that is NOT mentioned specifically as a change that may be required by or result from the introduction of group counseling in an adult correctional institution is a change in the 24.____

A. attitude of the institution's classification officers toward their own procedures in treating inmates
B. attitudes of the institution's psychologists toward correction officers
C. place where the treatment program is planned and from which it is directed
D. principal place where the psychological treatment program makes actual contact with the inmate

25. According to the above paragraph, under a program of group counseling in an adult correctional institution, treatment of inmates takes place 25.____

A. as soon as they are admitted to the prison
B. chiefly in the clinical center
C. mainly where inmates are in continuing close and personal relationship with the technical staff
D. wherever inmates come in contact with prison employees

KEY (CORRECT ANSWERS)

1. C
2. B
3. C
4. C
5. C
6. B
7. B
8. A
9. C
10. C
11. B
12. D
13. A
14. B
15. C
16. D
17. B
18. C
19. D
20. B
21. D
22. A
23. D
24. C
25. D

READING COMPREHENSION
UNDERSTANDING AND INTERPRETING WRITTEN MATERIAL
EXAMINATION SECTION
TEST 1

DIRECTIONS: Each question or incomplete statement is followed by several suggested answers or completions. Select the one that BEST answers the question or completes the statement. *PRINT THE LETTER OF THE CORRECT ANSWER IN THE SPACE AT THE RIGHT.*

Questions 1-4.

DIRECTIONS: Questions 1 through 4 are to be answered SOLELY on the basis of the following passage.

Morally, there is no basis for the assertion that the commission of a social offense allows society to strip a human being of all his rights except those which, through some sort of *natural law* concept, he needs to survive. Rather, society is justified in punishing offenders only to the extent that it needs to protect itself; excessive retribution is *immoral.* Thus, unless society can demonstrate that a specific deprivation is necessary to its self-preservation, or to its reassertion of authority over the individual offender, it should not be entitled to enforce the deprivation. To place the burden on the prisoner to demonstrate that he should not be deprived of a particular right appears to be unfair and unjustified for two reasons: (1) the resources and skills are unequally distributed in society's favor, and (2) the concept of *proportionality* as a rudimentary value is rejected by such an approach, which even theories of retribution and vengeance do not support.

Pragmatically, too, prisoners should be viewed and treated as human beings. Ninety-five percent of all those incarcerated in prisons are returned to the free world. It violates common sense to expect a man who has been treated at best as a cipher while in prison to be enamored of a society which has not only enchained him but also has increased his torment while he is confined. When he is released, his action is likely to be antisocial rather than social. Additionally, the imposition of excessive suffering on offenders permeates society's attitudes toward others in its midst. Just as we are now realizing that violence abroad erodes the barriers against domestic violence, official hostility toward some human beings tends to add an aura of authority to hostility toward and among others. Disinclination to cherish humanity at one point in society leads to total abdication of humanity at another.

1. In the above passage, it is pointed out that 1.____

   A. it is a practical approach to treatment to take away all but the basic rights of a prisoner
   B. it is proper to remove an inmate's rights within a system of rewards and punishments
   C. incarceration should not be used for revenge against one who has offended society
   D. the inmate ought to play a primary role in determining treatment methods

2. According to the above passage, 2.____

A. inmates who are treated badly are apt to resort to antisocial behavior when they are returned to society
B. there is a tendency among inmates to join organizations dedicated to achieving civil rights for the victims of society
C. society generally sees all inmates as being equal, despite inconsistent observation of prisoners' rights
D. recidivism is a serious problem for the majority of prisoners who are released on parole

3. While criticizing the kind of treatment prisoners receive in our institutions, the above passage implies that 3.____

A. the mistreatment of prisoners is an outcome of society's benign attitude toward the law-abiding citizen
B. cruelty begets cruelty, and that humane treatment will make better citizens of those entrusted to our care
C. when violence in this country spreads, it increases all over the world
D. an aura of authority has replaced official hostility in correctional institutions

4. According to the above passage, penal authorities are justified in depriving prisoners of rights 4.____

A. in order to satisfy society's desire for retribution against criminal offenders
B. until prisoners can demonstrate that particular deprivations are unjustified
C. whenever the preservation of order within the institution will be facilitated
D. only when it is necessary to protect society or maintain control over the inmate

Questions 5-8.

DIRECTIONS: Questions 5 through 8 are to be answered SOLELY on the basis of the following excerpt from a memo circulated by a correction official for comments.

Some bargaining is virtually inevitable between those charged with enforcing institutional regulations and inmates who are supposed to be regulated for the simple reason that administrators rarely have sufficient resources to gain complete conformity to all the rules. An insufficient number of guards and cells and inadequately threatening punishments create an environment in which institutional rules are often ignored. At the same time, the attempt to impose order upon individuals deprived of normal amenities, who often lack opportunities for adequate recreation or privacy, tends to produce violent disorder. Toleration by correctional administrators and officers of constant violation of institutional rules results even if confined to a level considered by administrators to be neither very visible nor very serious. Recurring contact between guards and inmates creates ample opportunity for an ongoing informal bargaining.

Although some form of bargaining has long been recognized as a basic process of control within prisons and other total institutions, it is not clear whether a system of control which relies on private, particularized bargains between staff and inmates contributes to the goals of rehabilitation, order, or protection from arbitrary punishment. In fact, within the daily bargaining process, often the only goal sought to be achieved by the institution is short term surface order - the semblance that everything is running smoothly with no official (or public) cause for alarm.

5. According to the above passage, all of the following conditions contribute to the existence of bargaining EXCEPT 5.____

   A. difficulty in getting inmates to conform to the rules
   B. the scarcity of guards and cells
   C. the scarcity of administrators
   D. the pressures of confinement brought on by prison conditions

6. According to the above passage, which one of the following is MOST likely to create a climate for bargaining between inmates and staff? 6.____

   A. Lack of privacy
   B. Lack of opportunities for recreation
   C. Frequent interaction between guards and inmates
   D. Desires of guards to avoid enforcement of rules

7. The author IMPLIES that the practice of bargaining in institutions is a process which 7.____

   A. is not generally recognized outside institutions
   B. eliminates violent disorders among inmates
   C. should be utilized more frequently
   D. has been in existence for a long time

8. According to the above passage, which one of the following statements concerning bargaining is MOST NEARLY correct? 8.____
   It

   A. contributes to the goals of the institution because it protects inmates from arbitrary punishment
   B. impedes rehabilitation since it weakens respect for correctional personnel
   C. is a method of reducing the visibility of inmate rule violations
   D. detracts from the smooth operation of the institution because it is an ineffective system of control

Questions 9-12.

DIRECTIONS: Questions 9 through 12 are to be answered on the basis of the following portion of a report submitted by a Tour Commander to the appropriate superior about an unusual occurrence in a Detention Dormitory. The portion of the report consists of 21 numbered sentences, some of which may or may not follow the principles of good report writing.

1. Following is a report of an altercation between inmate John Doe, #441-77-9375, and inmate Henry Green, #441-77-1656.
2. At approximately 6:15 A.M. on June 15, an alarm was received in the Control Room from Officer Arthur Kinney #6214 of the 7M dormitory (General Population).
3. Captain Ronald Doaks #529 and Officer Henry James #7654 responded immediately to determine the cause of the alarm.
4. Captain Doaks reports that, upon arrival, he observed inmate John Doe, #441-77-9375, on the officer's bridge bleeding from the mouth.

5. The institutional doctor also found a stab wound in the left arm.
6. The Captain observed inmate Henry Green, #441-77-1656, locked behind the *B* gate, heard him shouting obscenities and threatening further harm to Officer Kinney.
7. He noticed a large group of inmates standing quietly in the day room.
8. Officer Kinney, who was on post alone, reports he heard a commotion in the rear of the dormitory while sitting at his desk reading the Departmental Rules and Regulations.
9. He could not see what was going on because of a large crowd of inmates.
10. He reports that inmate Doe suddenly broke through the crowd screaming toward the *B* gate.
11. Doe was being pursued by inmate Green.
12. Officer Kinney states that he sounded the alarm and allowed inmate Doe onto the bridge.
13. Since inmate Doe was bleeding from the mouth, Captain Doaks ordered Officer James to escort him to the clinic for immediate examination and treatment by Dr. James White, who subsequently suspected a broken jaw and also discovered a puncture wound in the left bicep.
14. Dr. White ordered his transfer to Harmony Hospital for x-ray of the jaw.
15. Inmate Green, who appeared free of injury, stated to the Captain that he and Doe argued over the telephone, agreed to *take it to the back* and fight.
16. Green would make no further statements.
17. No other inmate in the dormitory would admit seeing anything.
18. Inmate Green received an infraction and was transferred to the Administrative Area pending further investigation.
19. The housing area was then restored to order and normal operations were resumed.
20. Prior to his transfer to the hospital, inmate Doe stated to the Captain that he was assaulted by inmate Green for no apparent reason.
21. He was told that he has an infraction and, upon return from the hospital, would be transferred to another housing unit pending investigation.

9. Of the following, which sentence is MOST likely to be out of sequence? 9.____

A. 2 B. 5 C. 8 D. 14

10. Of the following, which sentence indicates the GREATEST need for further clarification by the Tour Commander submitting the report? 10.____

A. 4 B. 6 C. 9 D. 17

11. Which one of the following sentences BEST indicates the possibility of potential danger remaining in 7M because of the omission of a necessary procedure? 11.____

A. 3 B. 14 C. 19 D. 21

12. Which one of the following sentences is LEAST significant to the report? 12.____

A. 4 B. 7 C. 11 D. 17

Questions 13-16.

DIRECTIONS: Questions 13 through 16 are to be answered SOLELY on the basis of the following fictitious directive which may or may not conform with actual policy and procedure of the Department of Correction.

DIRECTIVE NO. 15 Dated March 1

Guidelines for Members of the Department when accepting packages for inmates being held in custody of the City Department of Correction.

1. Receipt and Distribution of Packages

All packages delivered by the postal authorities must bear the name and address of the sender. All packages regardless of whether received through the mail or delivered by an individual, during visiting hours only, must be in a cardboard box with tape sealing same so as to prevent access to contents of package. When package is received by mail, it is to be placed in the mailroom of the institution concerned by the staff member assigned to picking up the mail. In addition, the officer delivering the package to mailroom officer will get a receipt for all packages. The mailroom officer shall prepare Form P-103 in duplicate, which will document the time and description of all packages received, including the contents thereof, as well as the name and address of the sender. Packages must be weighed and weight noted on Form P-103, as no inmate is to receive an excess of 40 lbs. in packages in a six-month period. Log is to be maintained of all packages received, distributed, and returned to sender, including the weights for packages received and accepted. When a package is brought to the institution by an individual, during visiting hours only, it is to bear the name and address of person who is responsible for articles in package, who must be the individual who is delivering the package. Form P-103 is to remain with package until signed by inmate, since original of Form P-103 is the institutional record and substantiation that inmate has received his/her package.

As soon as practicable, all packages are to be searched for contraband and appropriate actions taken. If package is determined to be acceptable, inmate concerned shall be called to mailroom and shall inspect package, sign Form P-103 in duplicate, receive the duplicate copy of Form P-103, and remove package to his/her respective cell. If the inmate is not available when called for, package is to be secured in a locked closet or room and key so secured that only authorized personnel have access to area. If mailroom officer is not on duty when package is brought to institution by an individual, officer assigned to visits is to be responsible for handling and safekeeping of package according to this directive.

2. Acceptability of Articles

Suitable clothing may be accepted in all packages according to guidelines determined by the head of each institution. However, the institutional clothing card must be referred to so excess clothing is not accumulated and in order to maintain a strict control over same. Food and snacks are also acceptable items - no alcoholic beverages, nor glass containers are to be accepted. Sharp instruments are not to be accepted nor any item that may create a hazard or breach of security within the institution. Shaving utensils are to be distributed by the institution and are not to be accepted in packages. Under no circumstances is money or jewelry to be accepted in packages. No medications are to be accepted when included in packages or otherwise, but, when the occasion arises, inmate must be instructed that all medications are dispensed through the medical staff assigned to that institution. Prescription eyeglasses can be accepted, but must be inspected and approved by the institutional physician before distribution to inmate. Under no circumstances are cigarettes to be accepted in packages since they must be purchased through each institutional commissary.

3. Appropriate Areas For Use

Food received in packages cannot be removed from the housing area. Under no circumstances should an inmate bring food to the main dining room as a substitution or addition to the departmental menu. Books and magazines cannot be removed from the housing areas. Under no condition should any inmate's library privileges be cancelled or modified because he has received publications from another source. All eatable items are to be consumed either in the inmate's cell or the day room of the housing area he/she is assigned to. Any inmate who has received special permission to receive an item of clothing for sporting or athletic purposes may use said clothing only in the gymnasium of the institution, said clothing is to remain in the gymnasium, and a system for laundering determined and controlled by the Recreation Director.

4. A. Safeguarding Undelivered Packages

All undelivered packages will be secured in a locked closet of the mailroom or the mailroom itself. The mailroom shall be secured whenever a custodial member is not in attendance. The key to the mailroom must be secured so that only authorized personnel have access to the area. The schedule for the use of the mailroom must be arranged to create accountability for the safekeeping of all packages received for any inmate of the Department. Every effort must be made to deliver packages to inmates as soon as is practicable. However, if after ten days, the package is not delivered, it must be returned to the sender with an appropriate notation - under no condition may a package remain undelivered for more than ten days.

B. Ensuring that Unacceptable Packages or Unacceptable Items Are Returned to Sender

All unacceptable packages or unacceptable items must be returned to sender immediately upon being determined unacceptable. The inmate must be notified of any article or package that is being returned, but not necessarily before the items have been mailed. Upon mailing any unacceptable items to the sender, no items shall be returned which would violate postal regulations. Whenever articles are returned to sender, a return receipt must be requested of the postal authorities.

5. Procedure for the Prosecution of Persons Violating the Postal Regulations or Prison Contraband Law

Whenever serious contraband is found in a package received by mail at an institution of the Department, the supervisor investigating the incident will notify the postal authorities, cooperating with them whenever possible. The officer who actually finds contraband must be witness to any criminal proceedings that would follow. If contraband is delivered to the institution by an individual, the Police Department shall be notified, and the supervisor investigating said incident will cooperate fully with the Police Department. The officer who actually finds contraband will be a witness if any criminal proceeding is instituted. All serious contraband will be turned over to the Police Department and a voucher received for same. The supervisor will conduct a complete investigation of all discoveries of serious contraband received in packages, and submit proper reports to the head of the institution.

6. System of Appeals for Those Inmates Denied Packages or Contents Thereof

Any inmate who has been denied a package or any article included in a package and has been informed of this by the mailroom officer may request Form P-111, fill out same, and return it to the mailroom officer. This is a form of appeal and must be forwarded to the A/D/W-A/D/S in charge of security, who will investigate the complaint and render a decision on the complaint. The inmate must be interviewed by the A/D/W or A/D/S or a designated person, who will inform him/her of the reason for the denial, and the security Deputy's decision. If the inmate tells the security Deputy he/she wishes to appeal, a copy of the decision and Form P-111 will be forwarded to the D/S or D/W for a final decision. If no appeal is requested after the interview and rendering of the A/D/W-A/D/S - decision, or at the conclusion or final decision by the D/W - D/S, Form P-111 and the written copy of the decision will be filed in the inmate's folder.

7. Procedure for Receiving Special Permission for Items or Articles Not Generally Allowed the Institutional Population, Before the Package is Received

An inmate wishing to receive a specific item who has a legitimate need, may write to the head of the institution stating the need, if the item is not generally allowed in the institution. When determined necessary by the head of the institution, the inmate will be asked to submit a professional opinion substantiating the need. The request and substantiation will be submitted to a review board and their determination will be forwarded to the head of the institution for his/her approval. Only upon receipt of the approval of the head of the institution will special permission be given for possession of a specific item or article.

13. According to the above directive, which one of the following is NOT a condition for receiving a package in an institution of the Department? 13.____

A. All packages must be weighed and logged in an effort to control the aggregate weight of packages received by each inmate at an institution.
B. Packages may be brought to the institution by individuals during visiting hours only.
C. If a package has been determined acceptable by a custodial officer, the inmate shall inspect the package, sign for it, and take possession of it.
D. The log maintained by the mailroom officer is the institutional substantiation that the inmate has received the package.

14. According to the above directive, which one of the following is NOT a valid statement regarding acceptability of items in packages received for inmates in institutions of the Department? 14.____

A. Money, jewelry, and medications are not to be accepted in packages.
B. Prescription eyeglasses can be accepted by the institution before they are approved and inspected by the institutional physician.
C. Shaving utensils which meet the guidelines established by the head of the institution may be acceptable when received in packages.
D. The institutional clothing card must be consulted when determining whether to accept clothing in packages.

15. According to the above directive, which one of the following statements is NOT valid concerning actions to be taken when postal regulations or prison contraband laws are violated while sending or delivering packages to an institution? 15.____

A. The officer who discovers serious contraband in a package, whether delivered to an institution by an individual or mailed through the postal authorities, is a witness as far as the Department is concerned.
B. The supervisor responsible for investigating the discovery of serious contraband in a package brought to the institution by a visitor must notify the Director of Operations immediately.
C. All serious contraband must be turned over to the Police Department and vouchered, whether or not criminal proceedings are instituted.
D. The supervisor responsible for investigating the discovery of serious contraband in a package brought to the institution must submit his/her report to the head of the institution.

16. According to the above directive, which one of the following is a VALID statement concerning an application for special permission to receive an article not generally allowed in an institution? 16.____

A. A professional opinion substantiating the need for the item requested must accompany the application for special permission to receive said item.
B. A review board, upon receipt of the application and professional opinion substantiating the need for the item, will render a final decision.
C. An inmate wishing to receive a special item, for any reason, may write to the head of the institution.
D. The head of the institution may approve, for use by a specific inmate, a specific item or article which is not generally permitted in the institution.

Questions 17-19.

DIRECTIONS: Questions 17 through 19 are to be answered SOLELY on the basis of the following passage.

In collaboration with operating staff and research social scientists, the statistician should be responsible for installing standard measures of achievement in the information system. Reliability of measurements used by the system should be reviewed periodically. This review will be especially important if predictive devices are installed to facilitate comparison of expectations with observed outcomes.

This evaluation technique is well suited to standardized use by information systems. A standard base expectancy table is established to predict results of programs for groups, using criteria such as recidivism or completion of training. Such a device will be capable of assigning any given subject to a class of like subjects grouped by the statistical weighting of aggregated characteristics. Group expectancy for success or failure as determined by recidivism or other criteria can be expressed in percentiles.

Use of base expectancies for comparison with observed outcomes may be thought of as a *soft* method of evaluation. But its economy, in comparison with the classical control group procedure, is considerable. It eliminates the need for routine management of research controls over extended periods. Comparison of predicted with observed outcome affords a rough estimate of program effectiveness. For example, if the average expected recidivism of a group of offenders exposed to a behavior modification program is 50 percent, but the observed outcome is 25 percent, a *prima facie* indication of program effectiveness is established.

Such an indication affords the administrator some assurance that a program seriously subjected to a controlled evaluation with similar results is continuing to be effective. It may also provide a rough estimate of the value of a program that has not been evaluated under the control group method. This kind of evaluation has many limitations. A predictive device is valid only to the extent that the group observed is typical of the population used as the basis for the standard. A second objection to the use of predictive devices in evaluation rests on the tendency of the predictive bases to deteriorate. The applicability of a prediction under circumstances prevailing in year one will not necessarily be the same circumstance prevailing in year ten. Accordingly, it is good practice to audit the accuracy of the predictive device at least every five years to assure that the circumstances are the same. A final objection is that predictive devices can be used only for global indications of program effectiveness.

17. Of the following, the KEY element in the traditional approach to program evaluation that would NOT be used in the approach described in the passage is 17.____

A. computers
B. recidivism rates
C. standard populations
D. control groups

18. Of the following, the MOST appropriate title for the above passage is 18.____

A. HOW TO PREDICT THE RESULTS OF PROGRAM EVALUATIONS
B. A *SOFT* METHOD OF PROGRAM EVALUATION
C. THE USE OF PREDICTIVE DEVICES IN PROGRAM EVALUATION
D. COOPERATION BETWEEN THE STATISTICIAN AND OPERATING STAFF

19. All of the following statements describe limitations of using predictive devices to evaluate programs for the first time EXCEPT: 19.____

A. The group under study must be typical of the group used to develop the predictive device.
B. Predictive devices can be used only for global indications of program effectiveness.
C. Predictive devices are more expensive to use than classical control group procedure.
D. The circumstances prevailing in the year of the study must be the same as in the year the predictive device was developed.

Questions 20-25.

DIRECTIONS: Questions 20 through 25 are to be answered SOLELY on the basis of the following passage.

At present, in State X, whole classes of offenders are retained at unnecessarily close and expensive levels of confinement and supervision because the various decision-makers involved are required to make predictions about the future behavior of offenders which cannot, given the present state of social science, be made accurately. Items such as social and psychological history, changes in attitude, estimates of institutional progress, and anticipation of constructive responses to parole supervision are particularly useless as evaluative criteria in the disposition of offenders because such subjective evaluations are rooted in the attitudes of the appraiser and in the constructive tendencies of bureaucracies.

The result has been that while probation is used extensively (chiefly because institutions are overcrowded) parole board policy has become increasingly cautious and expensive. Although the initial choice between probation and commitment to prison is often arbitrary, the offender thus committed tends to remain incarcerated for long periods. Because the absence of a clear, positive, and legislatively authorized parole policy is a fundamental obstacle to the reallocation of funds, and because the decision problems involved are repeated at each level of the correctional system, the Committee on Criminal Penalties examined the state parole policy. It then presented model legislation which required that offenders committed to prison be automatically released to parole at expiration of the statutory minimum parole-eligible period (often only six months under present law), unless their individual histories contained substantial evidence of past serious violence. The resulting institutional savings were to be devoted chiefly to improving parole services and subsidies for improvements in local law enforcement agencies.

The basic intent of the legislation was to substitute clearly defined statutory ineligibility for release criteria based on the past actions of offenders for the present administratively defined eligibility criteria that necessarily rely on predictive data of highly questionable validity. By requiring the early release of any offender not shown to be clearly ineligible, the act would essentially remove responsibility for the disposition of doubtful cases from the parole authorities and return it to the courts.

20. Of the following, the MOST suitable title for the above passage is 20.___

A. THE REASONS FOR GRANTING PAROLE
B. THE COMMITTEE ON CRIMINAL PENALTIES
C. DECISION PROBLEMS IN CORRECTIONS
D. A NEW APPROACH IN PAROLE POLICY

21. According to the above passage, which of the following is NOT a true statement about the present correctional system in State X? 21.___

A. Many offenders are retained at unnecessarily close and expensive levels of confinement and supervision.
B. The offenders committed to prison tend to remain incarcerated for long periods.
C. Probation has become more and more extensive in application chiefly because institutions are overcrowded.
D. When reviewing cases, parole authorities often use objective criteria like the social and psychological history of inmates.

22. According to the above passage, one change from the present system of parole which would result from the enactment of the proposed system of parole is that 22.___

A. criminals could be paroled after the minimum parole eligibility period
B. offenders who committed serious violent acts would automatically be paroled after a specified amount of time
C. institutions would become overcrowded
D. responsibility for parole in doubtful cases would essentially be given to the court rather than the parole authorities

23. According to the proposed method of determining parole, an inmate would be paroled after a specified period 23.____

A. unless ineligible by administrative criteria
B. unless ineligible by specific legislative criteria
C. if eligible according to administrative criteria
D. if eligible according to specific legislative criteria

24. Under the proposed method of determining parole, parole would be granted or denied depending on the inmate's 24.____

A. past actions
B. present behavior
C. present psychological adjustment
D. probable future actions

25. According to the above passage, the one of the following that is NOT a primary reason why the Committee on Criminal Penalties presented the legislation described above was to 25.____

A. set objective criteria for parole
B. expedite the reallocation of funds
C. eliminate arbitrary commitment to prison
D. prevent overlong commitment of many inmates

KEY (CORRECT ANSWERS)

1.	C	11.	C
2.	A	12.	B
3.	B	13.	D
4.	D	14.	C
5.	C	15.	B
6.	C	16.	D
7.	D	17.	D
8.	C	18.	C
9.	B	19.	C
10.	B	20.	D

21. D
22. D
23. B
24. A
25. C

PREPARING WRITTEN MATERIAL

PARAGRAPH REARRANGEMENT COMMENTARY

The sentences that follow are in scrambled order. You are to rearrange them in proper order and indicate the letter choice containing the correct answer at the space at the right.

Each group of sentences in this section is actually a paragraph presented in scrambled order. Each sentence in the group has a place in that paragraph; no sentence is to be left out. You are to read each group of sentences and decide upon the best order in which to put the sentences so as to form a well-organized paragraph.

The questions in this section measure the ability to solve a problem when all the facts relevant to its solution are not given.

More specifically, certain positions of responsibility and authority require the employee to discover connection between events sometimes, apparently, unrelated. In order to do this, the employee will find it necessary to correctly infer that unspecified events have probably occurred or are likely to occur. This ability becomes especially important when action must be taken on incomplete information.

Accordingly, these questions require competitors to choose among several suggested alternatives, each of which presents a different sequential arrangement of the events. Competitors must choose the MOST logical of the suggested sequences.

In order to do so, they may be required to draw on general knowledge to infer missing concepts or events that are essential to sequencing the given events. Competitors should be careful to infer only what is essential to the sequence. The plausibility of the wrong alternatives will always require the inclusion of unlikely events or of additional chains of events which are NOT essential to sequencing the given events.

It's very important to remember that you are looking for the best of the four possible choices, and that the best choice of all may not even be one of the answers you're given to choose from.

There is no one right way to solve these problems. Many people have found it helpful to first write out the order of the sentences, as they would have arranged them, on their scrap paper before looking at the possible answers. If their optimum answer is there, this can save them some time. If it isn't, this method can still give insight into solving the problem. Others find it most helpful to just go through each of the possible choices, contrasting each as they go along. You should use whatever method feels comfortable and works for you.

While most of these types of questions are not that difficult, we've added a higher percentage of the difficult type, just to give you more practice. Usually there are only one or two questions on this section that contain such subtle distinctions that you're unable to answer confidently. And you then may find yourself stuck deciding between two possible choices, neither of which you're sure about.

EXAMINATION SECTION

TEST 1

DIRECTIONS: Each question consists of several sentences which can be arranged in a logical sequence. For each question, select the choice which places the numbered sentences in the MOST logical sequence. *PRINT THE LETTER OF THE CORRECT ANSWER IN THE SPACE AT THE RIGHT.*

1. I. A body was found in the woods. 1.____
   II. A man proclaimed innocence.
   III. The owner of a gun was located.
   IV. A gun was traced.
   V. The owner of a gun was questioned.
   The CORRECT answer is:
   A. IV, III, V, II, I B. II, I, IV, III, V C. I, IV, III, V, II
   D. I, III, V, II, IV E. I, II, IV, III, V

2. I. A man is in a hunting accident. 2.____
   II. A man fell down a flight of steps.
   III. A man lost his vision in one eye,
   IV. A man broke his leg.
   V. A man had to walk with a cane.
   The CORRECT answer is:
   A. II, IV, V, I, III B. IV, V, I, III, II C. III, I, IV, V, II
   D. I, III, V, II, IV E. I, III, II, IV, V

3. I. A man is offered a new job. 3.____
   II. A woman is offered a new job.
   III. A man works as a waiter.
   IV. A woman works as a waitress.
   V. A woman gives notice.
   The CORRECT answer is:
   A. IV, II, V, III, I B. IV, II, V, I, III C. II, IV, V, III, I
   D. III, I, IV, II, V E. IV, III, II, V, I

4. I. A train let the station late. 4.____
   II. A man was late for work.
   III. A man lost his job.
   IV. Many people complained because the train was late.
   V. There was a traffic jam.
   The CORRECT answer is:
   A. V, II, I, IV, III B. V, I, IV, II, III C. V, I, II, IV, III
   D. I, V, IV, II, III E. II, I, IV, V, III

5. I. The burden of proof as to each issue is determined before trial and remains upon the same party throughout the trial. 5.____
II. The jury is at liberty to believe one witness' testimony as against a number of contradictory witnesses.
III. In a civil case, the party bearing the burden of proof is required to prove his contention by a fair preponderance of the evidence.
IV. However, it must be noted that a fair preponderance of evidence does not necessarily mean a greater number of witnesses.
V. The burden of proof is the burden which rests upon one of the parties to an action to persuade the trier of the facts, generally the jury, that a proposition he asserts is true.
VI. If the evidence is equally balanced, or if it leaves the jury in such doubt as to be unable to decide the controversy either way, judgment must be given against the party upon whom the burden of proof rests.

The CORRECT answer is:
A. III. II, V, IV, I, VI B. I, II, VI, V, III, IV C. III, IV, V, I, II, VI
D. V, I, III, VI, IV, II E. I, V, III, VI, IV, II

6. I. If a parent is without assets and is unemployed, he cannot be convicted of the crime of non-support of a child. 6.____
II. The term *sufficient ability* has been held to mean sufficient financial ability.
III. It does not matter if his unemployment is by choice or unavoidable circumstances.
IV. If he fails to take any steps at all, he may be liable to prosecution for endangering the welfare of a child.
V. Under the penal law, a parent is responsible for the support of his minor child only if the parent is of *sufficient ability*.
VI. An indigent parent may meet his obligation by borrowing money or by seeking aid under the provisions of the Social Welfare Law.

The CORRECT answer is:
A. VI, I, V, III, II, IV B. I, III, V, II, IV, VI C. V, II, I, III, VI, IV
D. I, VI, IV, V, II, III E. II, V, I, III, VI, IV

7. I. Consider, for example, the case of a rabble rouser who urges a group of twenty people to go out and break the windows of a nearby factory. 7.____
II. Therefore, the law fills the indicated gap with the crime of *inciting to riot*.
III. A person is considered guilty of inciting to riot when he urges ten or more persons to engage in tumultuous and violent conduct of a kind likely to create public alarm.
IV. However, if he has not obtained the cooperation of at least four people, he cannot be charged with unlawful assembly.
V. The charge of inciting to riot was added to the law to cover types of conduct which cannot be classified as either the crime of *riot* or the crime of *unlawful assembly*.
VI. If he acquires the acquiescence of at least four of them, he is guilty of unlawful assembly even if the project does not materialize.

The CORRECT answer is:
A. III, V, I, VI, IV, II B. V, I, IV, VI, II, III C. III, IV, I, V, II, VI
D. V, I, IV, VI, III, II E. V, III, I, VI, IV, II

8. I. If, however, the rebuttal evidence presents an issue of credibility, it is for the jury to determine whether the presumption has, in fact, been destroyed. 8.____
II. Once sufficient evidence to the contrary is introduced, the presumption disappears from the trial.
III. The effect of a presumption is to place the burden upon the adversary to come forward with evidence to rebut the presumption.
IV. When a presumption is overcome and ceases to exist in the case, the fact or facts which gave rise to the presumption still remain.
V. Whether a presumption has been overcome is ordinarily a question for the court.
VI. Such information may furnish a basis for a logical inference.
The CORRECT answer is:
A. IV, VI, II, V, I, III B. III, II, V, I, IV, VI C. V, III, VI, IV, II, I
D. V, IV, I, II, VI, III E. II, III, V, I, IV, VI

9. I. An executive may answer a letter by writing his reply on the face of the letter itself instead of having a return letter typed. 9.____
II. This procedure is efficient because it saves the executive's time, the typist's time, and saves office file space.
III. Copying machines are used in small offices as well as large offices to save time and money in making brief replies to business letters.
IV. A copy is made on a copying machine to go into the company files, while the original is mailed back to the sender.
The CORRECT answer is:
A. I, II, IV, III B. I, IV, II, III C. III, I, IV, II D. III, IV, II, I

10. I. Most organizations favor one of the types but always include the others to a lesser degree. 10.____
II. However, we can detect a definite trend toward greater use of symbolic control.
III. We suggest that our local police agencies are today primarily utilizing material control.
IV. Control can be classified into three types: physical, material, and symbolic.
The CORRECT answer is:
A. IV, II, III, I B. II, I, IV, III C. III, IV, II, I D. IV, I, III, II

11. I. Project residents had first claim to this use, followed by surrounding neighborhood children. 11.____
II. By contrast, recreation space within the project's interior was found to be used more often by both groups.
III. Studies of the use of project grounds in many cities showed grounds left open for public use were neglected and unused, both by residents and by members of the surrounding community.
IV. Project residents had clearly laid claim to the play spaces, setting up and enforcing unwritten rules for use.
V. Each group, by experience, found their activities easily disrupted by other groups, and their claim to the use of space for recreation difficult to enforce.

The CORRECT answer is:

A. IV, V, I, II, III
B. V, II, IV, III, I
C. I, IV, III, II, V
D. III, V, II, IV, I

12. I. They do not consider the problems correctable within the existing subsidy formula and social policy of accepting all eligible applicants regardless of social behavior. 12.____

II. A recent survey, however, indicated that tenants believe these problems correctable by local housing authorities and management within the existing financial formula.

III. Many of the problems and complaints concerning public housing management and design have created resentment between the tenant and the landlord.

IV. This same survey indicated that administrators and managers do not agree with the tenants.

The CORRECT answer is:

A. II, I, III, IV
B. I, III, IV, II
C. III, II, IV, I
D. IV, II, I, III

13. I. In single-family residences, there is usually enough distance between tenants to prevent occupants from annoying one another. 13.____

II. For example, a certain small percentage of tenant families has one or more members addicted to alcohol.

III. While managers believe in the right of individuals to live as they choose, the manager becomes concerned when the pattern of living jeopardizes others' rights.

IV. Still others turn night into day, staging lusty entertainments which carry on into the hours when most tenants are trying to sleep.

V. In apartment buildings, however, tenants live so closely together that any misbehavior can result in unpleasant living conditions.

VI. Other families engage in violent argument.

The CORRECT answer is:

A. III, II, V, IV, VI, I
B. I, V, II, VI, IV, III
C. II, V, IV, I, III, VI
D. IV, II, V, VI, III, I

14. I. Congress made the commitment explicit in the Housing Act of 194, establishing as a national goal the realization of a *decent home and suitable environment for every American family*. 14.____

II. The result has been that the goal of decent home and suitable environment is still as far distant as ever for the disadvantaged urban family.

III. In spite of this action by Congress, federal housing programs have continued to be fragmented and grossly underfunded.

IV. The passage of the National Housing Act signaled a few federal commitment to provide housing for the nation's citizens.

The CORRECT answer is:

A. I, IV, III, II
B. IV, I, III, II
C. IV, I, II, III
D. II, IV, I, III

15. I. The greater expense does not necessarily involve *exploitation*, but it is often perceived as exploitative and unfair by those who are aware of the price differences involved, but unaware of operating costs. 15.____
    II. Ghetto residents believe they are *exploited* by local merchants, and evidence substantiates some of these beliefs.
    III. However, stores in low-income areas were more likely to be small independents, which could not achieve the economies available to supermarket chains and were, therefore, more likely to charge higher prices, and the customers were more likely to buy smaller-sized packages which are more expensive per unit of measure.
    IV. A study conducted in one city showed that distinctly higher prices were charged for goods sold in ghetto stores in other areas.

    The CORRECT answer is:
    A. IV, II, I, III B. IV, I, III, II C. II, IV, III, I D. II, III, IV, I

KEY (CORRECT ANSWERS)

1.	C	6.	C	11.	D
2.	E	7.	A	12.	C
3.	B	8.	B	13.	B
4.	B	9.	C	14.	B
5.	D	10.	D	15.	C

PREPARING WRITTEN MATERIAL

EXAMINATION SECTION

TEST 1

DIRECTIONS: Each question or incomplete statement is followed by several suggested answers or completions. Select the one that BEST answers the question or completes the statement. *PRINT THE LETTER OF THE CORRECT ANSWER IN THE SPACE AT THE RIGHT.*

1. The one of the following sentences which is LEAST acceptable from the viewpoint of correct usage is: 1.____
   A. The police thought the fugitive to be him.
   B. The criminals set a trap for whoever would fall into it.
   C. It is ten years ago since the fugitive fled from the city.
   D. The lecturer argued that criminals are usually cowards.
   E. The police removed four bucketfuls of earth from the scene of the crime.

2. The one of the following sentences which is LEAST acceptable from the viewpoint of correct usage is: 2.____
   A. The patrolman scrutinized the report with great care.
   B. Approaching the victim of the assault, two bruises were noticed by the patrolman.
   C. As soon as I had broken down the door, I stepped into the room.
   D. I observed the accused loitering near the building, which was closed at the time.
   E. The storekeeper complained that his neighbor was guilty of violating a local ordinance.

3. The one of the following sentences which is LEAST acceptable from the viewpoint of correct usage is: 3.____
   A. I realized immediately that he intended to assault the woman, so I disarmed him.
   B. It was apparent that Mr. Smith's explanation contained many inconsistencies.
   C. Despite the slippery condition of the street, he managed to stop the vehicle before injuring the child.
   D. Not a single one of them wish, despite the damage to property, to make a formal complaint.
   E. The body was found lying on the floor.

4. The one of the following sentences which contains NO error in usage is: 4.____
   A. After the robbers left, the proprietor stood tied in his chair for about two hours before help arrived.
   B. In the cellar I found the watchman's hat and coat.
   C. The persons living in adjacent apartments stated that they had heard no unusual noises.

D. Neither a knife or any firearms were found in the room.
E. Walking down the street, the shouting of the crowd indicated that something was wrong.

5. The one of the following sentences which contains NO error in usage is: 5.____
A. The policeman lay a firm hand on the suspect's shoulder.
B. It is true that neither strength nor agility are the most important requirement for a good patrolman.
C. Good citizens constantly strive to do more than merely comply the restraints imposed by society.
D. No decision was made as to whom the prize should be awarded.
E. Twenty years is considered a severe sentence for a felony.

6. Which of the following sentences is NOT expressed in standard English usage? 5.____
A. The victim reached a pay-phone booth and manages to call police headquarters.
B. By the time the call was received, the assailant had left the scene.
C. The victim has been a respected member of the community for the past eleven years.
D. Although the lighting was bad and the shadows were deep, the storekeeper caught sight of the attacker.
E. Additional street lights have since been installed, and the patrols have been strengthened.

7. Which of the following sentences is NOT expressed in standard English usage? 7.____
A. The judge upheld the attorney's right to question the witness about the missing glove.
B. To be absolutely fair to all parties is the jury's chief responsibility.
C. Having finished the report, a loud noise in the next room startled the sergeant.
D. The witness obviously enjoyed having played a part in the proceedings.
E. The sergeant planned to assign the case to whoever arrived first.

8. In which of the following sentences is a word misused? 8.____
A. As a matter of principle, the captain insisted that the suspect's partner be brought for questioning.
B. The principle suspect had been detained at the station house for most of the day.
C. The principal in the crime had no previous criminal record, but his closest associate had been convicted of felonies on two occasions.
D. The interest payments had been made promptly, but the firm had been drawing upon the principal for these payments.
E. The accused insisted that his high school principal would furnish him a character reference.

9. Which of the following statements is ambiguous? 9.____
   A. Mr. Sullivan explained why Mr. Johnson had been dismissed from his job.
   B. The storekeeper told the patrolman he had made a mistake.
   C. After waiting three hours, the patients in the doctor's office were sent home.
   D. The janitor's duties were to maintain the building in good shape and to answer tenants' complaints.
   E. The speed limit should, in my opinion, be raised to sixty miles an hour on that stretch of road.

10. In which of the following is the punctuation or capitalization faulty? 10.____
   A. The accident occurred at an intersection in the Kew Gardens section of Queens, near the bus stop.
   B. The sedan, not the convertible, was struck in the side.
   C. Before any of the patrolmen had left the police car received an important message from headquarters.
   D. The dog that had been stolen was returned to his master, John Dempsey, who lived in East Village.
   E. The letter had been sent to 12 Hillside Terrace, Rutland, Vermont 05702.

Questions 11-25.

DIRECTIONS: Questions 11 through 25 are to be answered in accordance with correct English usage; that is, standard English rather than nonstandard or substandard. Nonstandard and substandard English includes words or expressions usually classified as slang, dialect, illiterate, etc., which are not generally accepted as correct in current written communication. Standard English also requires clarity, proper punctuation and capitalization and appropriate use of words. Write the letter of the sentence NOT expressed in standard English usage in the space at the right.

11. A. There were three witnesses to the accident. 11.____
   B. At least three witnesses were found to testify for the plaintiff.
   C. Three of the witnesses who took the stand was uncertain about the defendant's competence to drive.
   D. Only three witnesses came forward to testify for the plaintiff.
   E. The three witnesses to the accident were pedestrians.

12. A. The driver had obviously drunk too many martinis before leaving for home. 12.____
   B. The boy who drowned had swum in these same waters many times before.
   C. The petty thief had stolen a bicycle from a private driveway before he was apprehended.
   D. The detectives had brung in the heroin shipment they intercepted.
   E. The passengers had never ridden in a converted bus before.

13. A. Between you and me, the new platoon plan sounds like a good idea. 13.____
B. Money from an aunt's estate was left to his wife and he.
C. He and I were assigned to the same patrol for the first time in two months.
D. Either you or he should check the front door of that store.
E. The captain himself was not sure of the witness's reliability.

14. A. The alarm had scarcely begun to ring when the explosion occurred. 14.____
B. Before the firemen arrived at the scene, the second story had been destroyed.
C. Because of the dense smoke and heat, the firemen could hardly approach the now-blazing structure.
D. According to the patrolman's report, there wasn't nobody in the store when the explosion occurred.
E. The sergeant's suggestion was not at all unsound, but no one agreed with him.

15. A. The driver and the passenger they were both found to be intoxicated. 15.____
B. The driver and the passenger talked slowly and not too clearly.
C. Neither the driver nor his passengers were able to give a coherent account of the accident.
D. In a corner of the room sat the passenger, quietly dozing.
E. the driver finally told a strange and unbelievable story, which the passenger contradicted.

16. A. Under the circumstances I decided not to continue my examination of the premises. 16.____
B. There are many difficulties now not comparable with those existing in 1960.
C. Friends of the accused were heard to announce that the witness had better been away on the day of the trial.
D. The two criminals escaped in the confusion that followed the explosion.
E. The aged man was struck by the considerateness of the patrolman's offer.

17. A. An assemblage of miscellaneous weapons lay on the table. 17.____
B. Ample opportunities were given to the defendant to obtain counsel.
C. The speaker often alluded to his past experience with youthful offenders in the armed forces.
D. The sudden appearance of the truck aroused my suspicions.
E. Her studying had a good affect on her grades in high school.

18. A. He sat down in the theater and began to watch the movie. 18.____
B. The girl had ridden horses since she was four years old.
C. Application was made on behalf of the prosecutor to cite the witness for contempt.
D. The bank robber, with his two accomplices, were caught in the act.
E. His story is simply not credible.

19. A. The angry boy said that he did not like those kind of friends. 19.____
    B. The merchant's financial condition was so precarious that he felt he must avail himself of any offer of assistance.
    C. He is apt to promise more than he can perform.
    D. Looking at the messy kitchen, the housewife felt like crying.
    E. A clerk was left in charge of the stolen property.

20. A. His wounds were aggravated by prolonged exposure to sub-freezing temperatures. 20.____
    B. The prosecutor remarked that the witness was not averse to changing his story each time he was interviewed.
    C. The crime pattern indicated that the burglars were adapt in the handling of explosives.
    D. His rigid adherence to a fixed plan brought him into renewed conflict with his subordinates.
    E. He had anticipated that the sentence would be delivered by noon.

21. A. The whole arraignment procedure is badly in need of revision. 21.____
    B. After his glasses were broken in the fight, he would of gone to the optometrist if he could.
    C. Neither Tom nor Jack brought his lunch to work.
    D. He stood aside until the quarrel was over.
    E. A statement in the psychiatrist's report disclosed that the probationer vowed to have his revenge.

22. A. His fiery and intemperate speech to the striking employees fatally affected any chance of a future reconciliation. 22.____
    B. The wording of the statute has been variously construed.
    C. The defendant's attorney, speaking in the courtroom, called the official a demagogue who contempuously disregarded the judge's orders.
    D. The baseball game is likely to be the most exciting one this year.
    E. The mother divided the cookies among her two children.

23. A. There was only a bed and a dresser in the dingy room. 23.____
    B. John was one of the few students that have protested the new rule.
    C. It cannot be argued that the child's testimony is negligible; it is, on the contrary, of the greatest importance.
    D. The basic criterion for clearance was so general that officials resolved any doubts in favor of dismissal.
    E. Having just returned from a long vacation, the officer found the city unbearably hot.

24. A. The librarian ought to give more help to small children. 24.____
    B. The small boy was criticized by the teacher because he often wrote careless.
    C. It was generally doubted whether the women would permit the use of her apartment for intelligence operations.
    D. The probationer acts differently every time the officer visits him.
    E. Each of the newly appointed officers has 12 years of service.

25. A. The North is the most industrialized region in the country. 25.____
B. L. Patrick Gray 3d, the bureau's acting director, stated that, while "rehabilitation is fine" for some convicted criminals, "it is a useless gesture for those who resist every such effort."
C. Careless driving, faulty mechanism, narrow or badly kept roads all play their part in causing accidents.
D. The childrens' books were left in the bus.
E. It was a matter of internal security; consequently, he felt no inclination to rescind his previous order.

KEY (CORRECT ANSWERS)

1.	C	11.	C
2.	B	12.	D
3.	D	13.	B
4.	C	14.	D
5.	E	15.	A
6.	A	16.	C
7.	C	17.	E
8.	B	18.	D
9.	B	19.	A
10.	C	20.	C

21. B
22. E
23. B
24. B
25. D

TEST 2

DIRECTIONS: Each question or incomplete statement is followed by several suggested answers or completions. Select the one that BEST answers the question or completes the statement. *PRINT THE LETTER OF THE CORRECT ANSWER IN THE SPACE AT THE RIGHT.*

Questions 1-6.

DIRECTIONS: Each of Questions 1 through 6 consists of a statement which contains a word (one of those underlined) that is either incorrectly used because it is not in keeping with the meaning the quotation is evidently intended to convey, or is misspelled. There is only one INCORRECT word in each quotation. Of the four underlined words, determine if the first one should be replaced by the word lettered A, the second replaced by the word lettered B, the third replaced by the word lettered C, or the fourth replaced by the word lettered D.

1. Whether one depends on fluorescent or artificial light or both, adequate standards should be maintained by means of systematic tests. 1.____
   A. natural B. safeguards C. established D. routine

2. A police officer has to be prepared to assume his knowledge as a social scientist in the community. 2.____
   A. forced B. role C. philosopher D. street

3. It is practically impossible to indicate whether a sentence is too long simply by measuring its length. 3.____
   A. almost B. tell C. very D. guessing

4. Strong leaders are required to organize a community for delinquency prevention and for dissemination of organized crime and drug addiction. 4.____
   A. tactics B. important C. control D. meetings

5. The demonstrators who were taken to the Criminal Courts building in Manhattan (because it was large enough to accommodate them), contended that the arrests were unwarranted. 5.____
   A. demonstraters B. Manhatten
   C. accomodate D. unwarranted

6. They were guaranteed a calm atmosphere, free from harassment, which would be conducive to quiet consideration of the indictments. 6.____
   A. guarenteed B. atmspher
   C. harassment D. inditements

Questions 7-11.

DIRECTIONS: Each of Questions 7 through 11 consists of a statement containing four words in capital letters. One of these words in capital letters is not in keeping with the meaning which the statement is evidently intended to carry. The four words in capital letters in each statement are reprinted after the statement. Print the capital letter preceding the one of the four words which does MOST to spoil the true meaning of the statement in the space at the right.

7. Retirement and pension systems are essential not only to provide employees with with a means of support in the future, but also to prevent longevity and CHARITABLE considerations from UPSETTING the PROMOTIONAL opportunities RETIRED members of the career service. 7.____
   A. charitable B. upsetting C. promotional D. retired

8. Within each major DIVISION in a properly set up public or private organization, provision is made so that each NECESSARY activity is CARED for and lines of authority and responsibility are clear-cut and INFINITE. 8.____
   A. division B. necessary C. cared D. infinite

9. In public service, the scale of salaries paid must be INCIDENTAL to the services rendered, with due CONSIDERATION for the attraction of the desired MANPOWER and for the maintenance of a standard of living COMMENSURATE with the work to be performed. 9.____
   A. incidental B. consideration
   C. manpower D. commensurate

10. An understanding of the AIMS of an organization by the staff will AID greatly in increasing the DEMAND of the correspondence work of the office, and will to a large extent DETERMINE the nature of the correspondence. 10.____
   A. aims B. aid C. demand D. determine

11. BECAUSE the Civil Service Commission strongly feels that the MERIT system is a key factor in the MAINTENANCE of democratic government, it has adopted as one of its major DEFENSES the progressive democratization of its own procedures in dealing with candidates for positions in the public service. 11.____
   A. Because B. merit C. maintenance D. defenses

Questions 12-14.

DIRECTIONS: Questions 12 through 14 consist of one sentence each. Each sentence contains an incorrectly used word. First, decide which is the incorrectly used word. Then, from among the options given, decide which word, when substituted for the incorrectly used word, makes the meaning of the sentence clear.

<u>EXAMPLE</u>:

The U.S. national income exhibits a pattern of long term deflection.
   A. reflection B. subjection C. rejoicing D. growth

The word *deflection* in the sentence does not convey the meaning the sentence evidently intended to convey. The word *growth* (Answer D), when substituted for the word *deflection*, makes the meaning of the sentence clear. Accordingly, the answer to the question is D.

12. The study commissioned by the joint committee fell compassionately short of the mark and would have to be redone. 12.____
    A. successfully B. insignificantly
    C. experimentally D. woefully

13. He will not idly exploit any violation of the provisions of the order. 13.____
    A. tolerate B. refuse C. construe D. guard

14. The defendant refused to be virile and bitterly protested service. 14.____
    A. irked B. feasible C. docile D. credible

Questions 15-25.

DIRECTIONS: Questions 15 through 25 consist of short paragraphs. Each paragraph contains one word which is INCORRECTLY used because it is NOT in keeping with the meaning of the paragraph. Find the word in each paragraph which is INCORRECTLY used and then select as the answer the suggested word which should be substituted for the incorrectly used word.

<u>SAMPLE QUESTION</u>:
In determining who is to do the work in your unit, you will have to decide just who does what from day to day. One of your lowest responsibilities is to assign work so that everybody gets a fair share and that everyone can do his part well.
A. new B. old C. important D. performance

EXPLANATION:
The word which is NOT in keeping with the meaning of the paragraph is *lowest*. This is the INCORRECTLY used word. The suggested word *important* would be in keeping with the meaning of the paragraph and should be substituted for *lowest*. Therefore, the CORRECT answer is choice C.

15. If really good practice in the elimination of preventable injuries is to be achieved and held in any establishment, top management must refuse full and definite responsibility and must apply a good share of its attention to the task. 15.____
    A. accept B. avoidable C. duties D. problem

16. Recording the human face for identification is by no means the only service performed by the camera in the field of investigation. When the trial of any issue takes place, a word picture is sought to be distorted to the court of incidents, occurrences, or events which are in dispute. 16.____
    A. appeals B. description C. portrayed D. deranged

17. In the collection of physical evidence, it cannot be emphasized too strongly that a haphazard systematic search at the scene of the crime is vital. Nothing must be overlooked. Often the only leads in a case will come from the results of this search. 17.____
    A. important
    B. investigation
    C. proof
    D. thorough

18. If an investigator has reason to suspect that the witness is mentally stable, or a habitual drunkard, he should leave no stone unturned in his investigation to determine if the witness was under the influence of liquor or drugs, or was mentally unbalanced either at the time of the occurrence to which he testified or at the time of the trial. 18.____
    A. accused B. clue C. deranged D. question

19. The use of records is a valuable step in crime investigation and is the main reason every department should maintain accurate reports. Crimes are not committed through the use of departmental records alone but from the use of all records, of almost every type, wherever they may be found and whenever they give any incidental information regarding the criminal. 19.____
    A. accidental B. necessary C. reported D. solved

20. In the years since passage of the Harrison Narcotic Act of 1914, making the possession of opium amphetamines illegal in most circumstances, drug use has become a subject of considerable scientific interest and investigation. There is at present a voluminous literature on drug use of various kinds. 20.____
    A. ingestion B. derivatives C. addiction D. opiates

21. Of course, the fact that criminal laws are extremely patterned in definition does not mean that the majority of persons who violate them are dealt with as criminals. Quite the contrary, for a great many forbidden acts are voluntarily engaged in within situations of privacy and go unobserved and unreported. 21.____
    A. symbolic B. casual C. scientific D. broad-gauged

22. The most punitive way to study punishment is to focus attention on the pattern of punitive action: to study how a penalty is applied, too study what is done to or taken from an offender. 22.____
    A. characteristic B. degrading C. objective D. distinguished

23. The most common forms of punishment in times past have been death, physical torture, mutilation, branding, public humiliation, fines, forfeits of property, banishment, transportation, and imprisonment. Although this list is by no means differentiated, practically every form of punishment has had several variations and applications. 23.____
    A. specific B. simple C. exhaustive D. characteristic

24. There is another important line of inference between ordinary and professional criminals, and that is the source from which they are recruited. The professional criminal seems to be drawn from legitimate employment and, in many instances, from parallel vocations or pursuits. 24.____
    A. demarcation B. justification C. superiority D. reference

25. He took the position that the success of the program was insidious on getting additional revenue. 25.____
    A. reputed B. contingent C. failure D. indeterminate

KEY (CORRECT ANSWERS)

1.	A	11.	D
2.	B	12.	D
3.	B	13.	A
4.	C	14.	C
5.	D	15.	A
6.	C	16.	C
7.	D	17.	D
8.	D	18.	C
9.	A	19.	D
10.	C	20.	B

21. D
22. C
23. C
24. A
25. B

TEST 3

DIRECTIONS: Each question or incomplete statement is followed by several suggested answers or completions. Select the one that BEST answers the question or completes the statement. *PRINT THE LETTER OF THE CORRECT ANSWER IN THE SPACE AT THE RIGHT.*

Questions 1-5.

DIRECTIONS: Questions 1 through 5 are to be answered on the basis of the following.

You are a supervising officer in an investigative unit. Earlier in the day, you directed Detectives Tom Dixon and Sal Mayo to investigate a reported assault and robbery in a liquor store within your area of jurisdiction.

Detective Dixon has submitted to you a preliminary investigative report containing the following information:

- At 1630 hours on 2/20, arrived at Joe's Liquor Store at 350 SW Avenue with Detective Mayo to investigate A & R.
- At store interviewed Rob Ladd, store manager, who stated that he and Joe Brown (store owner) had been stuck up about ten minutes prior to our arrival.
- Ladd described the robbers as male whites in their late teens or early twenties. Further stated that one of the robbers displayed what appeared to be an automatic pistol as he entered the store, and said, *Give us the money or we'll kill you.* Ladd stated that Brown then reached under the counter where he kept a loaded .38 caliber pistol. Several shots followed, and Ladd threw himself to the floor.
- The robbers fled, and Ladd didn't know if any money had been taken.
- At this point, Ladd realized that Brown was unconscious on the floor and bleeding from a head wound.
- Ambulance called by Ladd, and Brown was removed by same to General Hospital.
- Personally interviewed John White, 382 Dartmouth Place, who stated he was inside store at the time of occurrence. White states that he hid behind a wine display upon hearing someone say, *Give us the money.* He then heard shots and saw two young men run from the store to a yellow car parked at the curb. White was unable to further describe auto. States the taller of the two men drove the car away while the other sat on passenger side in front.
- Recovered three spent .38 caliber bullets from premises and delivered them to Crime Lab.
- To General Hospital at 1800 hours but unable to interview Brown, who was under sedation and suffering from shock and a laceration of the head.
- Alarm #12487 transmitted for car and occupants.
- Case Active.

Based solely on the contents of the preliminary investigation submitted by Detective Dixon, select one sentence from the following groups of sentences which is MOST accurate and is grammatically correct.

1. A. Both robbers were armed. 1.____
   B. Each of the robbers were described as a male white.
   C. Neither robber was armed.
   D. Mr. Ladd stated that one of the robbers was armed.

2. A. Mr. Brown fired three shots from his revolver. 2.____
   B. Mr. Brown was shot in the head by one of the robbers.
   C. Mr. Brown suffered a gunshot wound of the head during the course of the robbery.
   D. Mr. Brown was taken to General Hospital by ambulance.

3. A. Shots were fired after one of the robbers said, *Give us the money or we'll kill you.* 3.____
   B. After one of the robbers demanded the money from Mr. Brown, he fired a shot.
   C. The preliminary investigation indicated that although Mr. Brown did not have a license for the gun, he was justified in using deadly physical force.
   D. Mr. Brown was interviewed at General Hospital.

4. A. Each of the witnesses were customers in the store at the time of occurrence. 4.____
   B. Neither of the witnesses interviewed was the owner of the liquor store.
   C. Neither of the witnesses interviewed were the owner of the store.
   D. Neither of the witnesses was employed by Mr. Brown.

5. A. Mr. Brown arrived at General Hospital at about 5:00 P.M. 5.____
   B. Neither of the robbers was injured during the robbery.
   C. The robbery occurred at 3:30 P.M. on February 10.
   D. One of the witnesses called the ambulance.

Questions 6-10.

DIRECTIONS: Each of Questions 6 through 10 consists of information given in outline form and four sentences labeled A, B, C, and D. For each question, choose the one sentence which CORRECTLY expresses the information given in outline form and which also displays PROPER English usage.

6. Client's Name: Joanna Jones 6.____
   Number of Children: 3
   Client's Income: None
   Client's Marital Status: Single

   A. Joanna Jones is an unmarried client with three children who have no income.
   B. Joanna Jones, who is single and has no income, a client she has three children.
   C. Joanna Jones, whose three children are clients, is single and has no income.
   D. Joanna Jones, who has three children, is an unmarried client with no income.

7. Client's Name: Bertha Smith 7.____
Number of Children: 2
Client's Rent: $1050 per month
Number of Rooms: 4

A. Bertha Smith, a client, pays $1050 per month for her four rooms with two children.
B. Client Bertha Smith has two children and pays $1050 per month for four rooms.
C. Client Bertha Smith is paying $1050 per month for two children with four rooms.
D. For four rooms and two children client Bertha Smith pays $1050 per month.

8. Name of Employee: Cynthia Dawes 8.____
Number of Cases Assigned: 9
Date Cases were Assigned: 12/16
Number of Assigned Cases Completed: 8

A. On December 16, employee Cynthia Dawes was assigned nine cases; she has completed eight of these cases.
B. Cynthia Dawes, employee on December 16, assigned nine cases, completed eight.
C. Being employed on December 16, Cynthia Dawes completed eight of nine assigned cases.
D. Employee Cynthia Dawes, she was assigned nine cases and completed eight, on December 16.

9. Place of Audit: Broadway Center 9.____
Names of Auditors: Paul Cahn, Raymond Perez
Date of Audit: 11/20
Number of Cases Audited: 41

A. On November 20, at the Broadway Center 41 cases was audited by auditors Paul Cahn and Raymond Perez.
B. Auditors Raymond Perez and Paul Cahn has audited 41 cases at the Broadway Center on November 20.
C. At the Broadway Center, on November 20, auditors Paul Cahn and Raymond Perez audited 41 cases.
D. Auditors Paul Cahn and Raymond Perez at the Broadway Center, on November 20, is auditing 41 cases.

10. Name of Client: Barbra Levine 10.____
Client's Monthly Income: $2100
Client's Monthly Expenses: $4520

A. Barbra Levine is a client, her monthly income is $2100 and her monthly expenses is $4520.
B. Barbra Levine's monthly income is $2100 and she is a client, with whose monthly expenses are $4520.

C. Barbra Levine is a client whose monthly income is $2100 and whose monthly expenses are $4520.
D. Barbra Levine, a client, is with a monthly income which is $2100 and monthly expenses which are $4520.

Questions 11-13.

DIRECTIONS: Questions 11 through 13 involve several statements of fact presented in a very simple way. These statements of fact are followed by 4 choices which attempt to incorporate all of the facts into one logical statement which is properly constructed and grammatically correct.

11. I. Mr. Brown was sweeping the sidewalk in front of his house. 11.____
II. He was sweeping it because it was dirty.
III. He swept the refuse into the street.
IV. Police Officer gave him a ticket.

Which one of the following BEST presents the information given above?
A. Because his sidewalk was dirty, Mr. Brown received a ticket from Officer Green when he swept the refuse into the street.
B. Police Officer Green gave Mr. Brown a ticket because his sidewalk was dirty and he swept the refuse into the street.
C. Police Officer Green gave Mr. Brown a ticket for sweeping refuse into the street because his sidewalk was dirty.
D. Mr. Brown, who was sweeping refuse from his dirty sidewalk into the street, was given a ticket by Police Officer Green.

12. I. Sergeant Smith radioed for help. 12.____
II. The sergeant did so because the crowd was getting larger.
III. It was 10:00 A.M. when he made his call.
IV. Sergeant Smith was not in uniform at the time of occurrence.

Which one of the following BEST presents the information given above?
A. Sergeant Smith, although not on duty at the time, radioed for help at 10 o'clock because the crowd was getting uglier.
B. Although not in uniform, Sergeant Smith called for help at 10:00 A.M. because the crowd was getting uglier.
C. Sergeant Smith radioed for help at 10:00 A.M. because the crowd was getting larger.
D. Although he was not in uniform, Sergeant Smith radioed for help at 10:00 A.M. because the crowd was getting larger.

13. I. The payroll office is open on Fridays. 13.____
II. Paychecks are distributed from 9:00 A.M. to 12 Noon.
III. The office is open on Fridays because that's the only day the payroll staff is available.
IV. It is open for the specified hours in order to permit employees to cash checks at the bank during lunch hour.

The choice below which MOST clearly and accurately presents the above idea is:

A. Because the payroll office is open on Fridays from 9:00 A.M. to 12 Noon, employees can cash their checks when the payroll staff is available.
B. Because the payroll staff is only available on Fridays until noon, employees can cash their checks during their lunch hour.
C. Because the payroll staff is available only on Fridays, the office is open from 9:00 A.M. to 12 Noon to allow employees to cash their checks.
D. Because of payroll staff availability, the payroll office is open on Fridays. It is open from 9:00 A.M. to 12 Noon so that distributed paychecks can be cashed at the bank while employees are on their lunch hour.

Questions 14-16.

DIRECTIONS: In each of Questions 14 through 6, the four sentences are from a paragraph in a report. They are not in the right order. Which of the following arrangements is the BEST one?

14. I. An executive may answer a letter by writing his reply on the face of the letter itself instead of having a return letter typed. 14.____
II. This procedure is efficient because it saves the executive's time, the typist's time, and saves office file space.
III. Copying machines are used in small offices as well as large offices to save time and money in making brief replies to business letters.
IV. A copy is made on a copy machine to go into the company files, while the original is mailed back to the sender.

The CORRECT answer is:
A. I, II, IV, III B. I, IV, II, III C. III, I, IV, II D. III, IV, II, I

15. I. Most organizations favor one of the types but always include the others to a lesser degree. 15.____
II. However, we can detect a definite trend toward greater use of symbolic control.
III. We suggest that our local police agencies are today primarily utilizing material control.
IV. Control can be classified into three types: physical, material, and symbolic.

The CORRECT answer is:
A. IV, II, III, I B. II, I, IV, III C. III, IV, II, I D. IV, I, III, II

16. I. They can and do take advantage of ancient political and geographical boundaries, which often give them sanctuary from effective policy activity. 16.____
II. This country is essentially a country of small police forces, each operating independently within the limits of its jurisdiction.
III. The boundaries that define and limit police operations do not hinder the movement of criminals, of course.
IV. The machinery of law enforcement in America is fragmented, complicated, and frequently overlapping.

The CORRECT answer is:
A. III, I, IV B. II, IV, I, III C. IV, II, III, I D. IV, III, II, I

17. Examine the following sentence, and then choose from below the words which should be inserted in the blank spaces to produce the best sentence. 17.____
The unit has exceeded _____ goals and the employees are satisfied with _____ accomplishments.
A. their, it's B. it's; it's C. its, there D. its, their

18. Examine the following sentence, and then choose from below the words which should be inserted in the blank spaces to produce the best sentence. 18.____
Research indicates that employees who _____ no opportunity for close social relationships often find their work unsatisfying, and this _____ of satisfaction often reflects itself in low production.
A. have; lack B. have; excess C. has; lack D. has; excess

19. Words in a sentence must be arranged properly to make sure that the intended meaning of the sentence is clear. 19.____
The sentence below that does NOT make sense because a clause has been separated from the word on which its meaning depends is:
A. To be a good writer, clarity is necessary.
B. To be a good writer, you must write clearly.
C. You must write clearly to be a good writer.
D. Clarity is necessary to good writing.

Questions 20-21.

DIRECTIONS: Each of Questions 20 and 21 consists of a statement which contains a word (one of those underlined) that is either incorrectly used because it is not in keeping with the meaning the quotation is evidently intended to convey, or is misspelled. There is only one INCORRECT word in each quotation. Of the four underlined words, determine if the first one should be replaced by the word lettered A, the second one replaced by the word lettered B, the third one replaced by the word lettered C, or the fourth one replaced by the word lettered D.

20. The alleged killer was occasionally permitted to excercise in the corridor. 20.____
A. alledged B. ocasionally C. permited D. exercise

21. Defense counsel stated, in affect, that their conduct was permissible under the First Amendment. 21.____
A. council B. effect C. there D. permissable

Question 22.

DIRECTIONS: Question 22 consists of one sentence. This sentence contains an incorrectly used word. First, decide which is the incorrectly used word. Then, from among the options given, decide which word, when substituted for the incorrectly used word, makes the meaning of the sentence clear.

22. As today's violence has no single cause, so its causes have no single scheme. 22.____
    A. deference B. cure C. flaw D. relevance

23. In the sentence, *A man in a light-grey suit waited thirty-five minutes in the ante-room for the all-important document*, the word IMPROPERLY hyphenated is 23.____
    A. light-grey
    B. thirty-five
    C. ante-room
    D. all-important

24. In the sentence, *The candidate wants to file his application for preference before it is too late*, the word *before* is used as a(n) 24.____
    A. preposition
    B. subordinating conjunction
    C. pronoun
    D. adverb

25. In the sentence, *The perpetrators ran from the scene*, the word *from* is a 25.____
    A. preposition B. pronoun C. verb D. conjunction

KEY (CORRECT ANSWERS)

1.	D	11.	D
2.	D	12.	D
3.	A	13.	D
4.	B	14.	C
5.	D	15.	D
6.	D	16.	C
7.	B	17.	D
8.	A	18.	A
9.	C	19.	A
10.	C	20.	D

21.	B
22.	B
23.	C
24.	B
25.	A

www.ingramcontent.com/pod-product-compliance
Lightning Source LLC
Chambersburg PA
CBHW082209300426
44117CB00016B/2735
* 9 7 8 1 7 9 9 3 0 9 5 7 4 *